To Dawn,

am amazing woman —
Embrace your Past
Live in your Present
+
Trust your Future!
Rev. Pina

STUCK IN THE PAST CAN GET YOU BURNED

STUCK IN THE PAST CAN GET YOU BURNED

DISCOVERING HOW TO LIVE IN THE PRESENT
WITHOUT THE PAIN OF YOUR PAST BY
GETTING UNSTUCK STEP BY STEP,
LEARNING TO WALK IN YOUR BLESSINGS

REVEREND DYANNE BLAIR-PINA

Foreword by Reverend Dr. David L. Kelley II

DEDICATED

To my amazing husband, Jeffrey who has been my rock,
to my beloved children, Corey, Janay and Blair
who love me in spite of myself, and to my siblings, Denise
and Randall, who like me, have thrived "against the odds."

CONTENTS

FOREWORD

This compelling book, penned by the Rev. Dyanne Blair-Pina, will become a valuable resource for a multitude of Christians who are seeking and searching for solutions and strength to overcome the many concealed horrors of life's secret and shameful dark problems of our past.

In the Protestant church we read past the admonition of James 5:16, *"Confess your trespasses to one another, and pray for one another, that you may be healed. The effective, fervent prayer of a righteous man avails much."* We fear the exposure and embarrassment of our secret scars and sins being told will become juicy subjects for the gossipmongers and fodder for public preaching illustrations so easily discerned by the average church listener. So we suffer in silence, in our sanctuaries, hiding our hurt and holding our pain close to our hearts, while hindering any expectation of ever receiving the healing, help, and hope that so many believers desperately need.

The journey through this book will offer a no-holds barred look at the life of one who has faced the ills of abandonment, alcoholism, abortion, abuse, mental illness, rejection, racism, drugs, death, denial, stress, tragedy, and a host of other psychological side effects of the socio-economic conditions of a life lived in the urban community of North America over the last half-century.

I applaud Rev. Blair-Pina for allowing readers a courageous and remarkably transparent look into the dark problems deeply embedded in the subconscious of her young soul. Now working in a life of ministry to help others, she has composed what I believe is a book that will minister to the body of Christ. Rev. Blair-Pina communicates clear, meaningful messages of liberation through biblical, life-lifting lessons as she delves into real and personal pain with clinical pastoral expertise that can lead to healing, help, and hope.

The poet laureate, Edgar Guest, wrote a poem titled, *"I'd Rather See a Sermon"* that speaks of what this book actually does for the reader.

> *I'd rather see a sermon than hear one any day:*
> *I'd rather one would walk with me than merely tell the way.*
> *The eye's a better pupil, and more willing than the ear,*
> *Fine counsel is confusing, but example's always clear.*
> *The best of all the preachers are men who live their creed,*
> *For to see good put into action, is what everyone needs.*
> *I can soon learn how to do it, if you let me see it done,*
> *I can catch your hands in action, but your tongue too fast may run.*
> *And the lecture you deliver may be very wise and true,*
> *But I'd rather get my lesson by observing what you do.*
> *For I may misunderstand you in the high advice you give,*
> *But there is no misunderstanding how you act and how you live.*
> *When I see an act of kindness, I am eager to be kind;*
> *When a weaker brother stumbles, and a stronger stays behind.*
> *Just to see if I can help him, then the wish grows strong in me,*
> *To be as big and thoughtful as I know that friend to be.*
> *And all travelers can witness that the best of guides today,*
> *Is not the one that tells them, but the one that shows the way.*

Rev. Blair-Pina has taken the testimony of her life and artfully and carefully given us a sermon we can see. The goal of preaching, more than any other goal, should be to minister to the needs of the people sitting in the pews. I believe this means ministering to the hurting masses who are 'Stuck in the Past' and who are silently roaring for a real redemptive word that will aid in reconciliation. Here is help that will allow the reader to face the past without fear of being burned but by taking the necessary steps that will lead to life bettered and blessed.

Walk on, my Sister, walk on!

—Rev. Dr. David Lawrence Kelley II
Senior Pastor
Christ Fellowship Baptist Church
Brooklyn, New York

INTRODUCTION

O Lord, you have searched me and you know me.

—PSALM 139:1

There is a saying that no one knows you better than yourself. I concur with this statement, and I disagree with this statement. I agree that not even a sibling twin knows its sibling like itself, or even a couple married 33 years knows the inner secrets or struggles of their spouse. Yet, in all of our own understanding of who we are or who we think we are, we still do not know ourselves like God knows us. I thank God for knowing me before I accepted Him as my Lord and Savior. I had no idea that there was a divine being that knew me intimately. I had no reason to seek intimacy with God. I grew up independently. Independence for me was a means to survival living in a household with addiction. Both of my parents were alcoholics and my dad was a gambler. In spite of my childhood, I was determined to do better... I did better and was the first in my family to graduate from college. Unfortunately, my mother never got to see me walk across the Boston University platform to receive my diploma; a year prior, she died of alcoholism.

It was not until I was twenty-three years old that I found out who this Jesus was. God had searched me and it was now my time to search and know him. My past pains and regrets were impacting my new Christian life with bitterness, anger and forgiveness. I was angry about my childhood. I felt jilted that I had to grow up very fast. I was bitter that my dad did not take care of us the way he should have. I could not forgive my mother for dying and missing out on all of the experiences that a mother should be present for. She was not there for my graduation, she was not there for my wedding, she was not there for my first birth, nor was she present for the many other joyful and sad moments in my life as a young woman.

My past became my prison. It would be another twenty-six years before I released my past and discovered what spiritual freedom felt like!

CHAPTER ONE

WHERE THERE'S SMOKE THERE'S FIRE

Now we know that if the earthly tent we live in is destroyed,
we have a building from God, and eternal house in heaven

—2 Corinthians 5:1

I was a child of the sixties and seventies and grew up in Roxbury, an urban neighborhood of Boston, Massachusetts. One of the most terrifying nights of my childhood occurred in the fall of 1966. I was six years old when we lived on the third floor of a three-family brownstone in the community of Roxbury. It was about three in the morning and everything was quiet, as it should have been. But, sometimes silence can be deadly. We did not hear the fire that was brewing within the apartment walls. Our neighbor on the first floor could not sleep and was knitting a blanket for her unborn child. Praise God she could not sleep. I call her our guardian angel because that night she banged on our door telling my parents she smelled smoke and to hurry out! It was an electrical fire inside the walls. Any moment the fire would rip through. I woke to my mother shaking me, "Get up, we have to go now!" She grabbed me. I was frightened and just scared to death. The next thing I knew we were on the stairwell, my mother clutching the hands of my younger brother and me. My older brother and sister were close behind brushing against my back. My dad was further behind because he refused to leave until he was dressed in pants and shirt. Not even in a fire would my dad come out in pajamas.

I recall my mother urging us to follow her, to keep moving and don't look back. I was so tempted to look back, to see if my dad was coming behind us. But, I resisted, and I obeyed, keeping my eyes straight ahead as we walked carefully down the dark stairwell, watching the smoke ooze from the walls. I'll never forget the fear, wondering when the flames would push through. It was terrifying. Thoughts raced through my young mind, "Was my daddy dead, would we soon burn to death, where was our dog Hobo?" And then before I realized, we were outside, the entire family, including Hobo.

We got out just in time. There we stood shivering in the cold night next to the fire truck, almost in shock watching the flames burst from the third floor balcony. It had only been a few months ago when my father had fallen off a ladder while on a painting job at an apartment building down the street. He almost died; and now we stand here cheating death again. We went to our cousin's house for the night and returned in the daylight to see what we could salvage. There was not much to retrieve after the damage of smoke, fire and water. We could not live there anymore. We had to look ahead. It was difficult to face and it would be unfamiliar, but it was time to move from that place…and so we did.

There is an Old Testament narrative in Genesis chapter 19, which echoes some of the lessons I gleaned from this dark and dangerous night. It is about the tragic story of the destruction of Sodom and Gomorrah, the cities of the plain that refused to obey God, living a lifestyle of self-indulgence.

The story within the story is about a husband's desperate fight to save his wife and children from the inevitable wrath of God's fire and brimstone. The patriarch was the key figure in the role and social structure of the Hebraic tribe, clan and family household. The fundamental family unit was the household or 'bet av', interpreted in Hebrew 'house of father'. It consisted of the responsible adult male, his wife, sons, and other dependents. Lineage was passed through sons, and married daughters joined the households of their husbands. Lot is the patriarch in this Genesis tragedy.

One morning early morning at dawn, the angels woke Lot, urging him to get up and take his wife and two daughters or he would be swept away and consumed in the punishment of the city. Lot was moving too slowly so the angels seized him and his family by the hand and brought them outside the city telling them to flee for their lives and do not look back; do not stop anywhere in the plain. Then the angels warned them for the second time, that if they did look back, they would be consumed!

I could identify with the sense of urgency in order to avoid death. I could identify with the commands of the angels..." Get up, wake up, do not look back, do not stop." These were the same imperatives my mother told me that night. In the middle of chaos, my mother was calm and focused. These were the earlier years before my mother befriended alcohol. She was in command and saved my family during that tragic night.

As a mother, I can relate to the many times I warned my children for their protection. As an African-American parent, my husband and I have had to prepare our two sons for the potential hazards of being a black male in this country. When they received their driver's licenses, I taught them how to behave and speak whenever that time came when a police officer would pull them over for no apparent reason other than the color of their skin. I had to teach them to not speak loudly or move suddenly in the presence of a police officer. When we moved to the suburbs, I taught them not to walk home alone when it was dark as they would be candidates for profiling, especially if they wore the hood of their sweatshirt. It was just a matter of time. My eldest son, who is now an Air Force Captain, was sixteen and had just completed a job application at a retail store with a friend. When he left the store, two policemen put them against the police car and asked for identification. My son handled the situation and was obedient. The officers did not handcuff or arrest them. I was angered by the insufficient response of the officer that these two boys looked like two others who robbed a store. As angry as I was for this poor excuse of an injustice, I counted my blessing that my son was not arrested, and I was grateful for his self-control and obedience. If he had reacted differently, things could have gone very badly.

Warnings of disobedience and its consequences are prevalent and necessary in our society. The media warns us "Don't Drink and Drive", "Don't Smoke", "Don't let your children talk to strangers". If taken lightly or dismissed, disobedience can result in death. The same went for Lot and his family. If they wanted to see their future, their only option was to be obedient and move swiftly. They did not move fast enough and God showed mercy through His emissaries or agents in the forms of angels who took drastic measures, grabbing him and his family to safety. I started to ponder over the idea of what would have happened if I looked back on that stairwell? My mother's wisdom says it all. She knew that if any of us looked back we could have lost our footing in the dark and stumbled, causing a domino effect with everyone falling. She knew there were only seconds to spare, or we could have been trapped in the fire as it breathed through the walls. *She knew that if we were consumed with looking back, we could have been consumed by the fire!*

When Lot warned his future sons-in-law to leave with him and his family because they would be consumed by the fire, they thought Lot was joking. The last laugh could have been on Lot because these young men perished in the fire. Lot's own wife looked back and turned into a pillar of salt...stuck in time, stuck forever in the past. The word "look" intrigued me. I was puzzled how maybe a glance, caused her to get stuck. After examining the Hebrew word in its grammatical context, I was no longer puzzled. The word "look" in Hebrew is nabat. In this passage, the verb is an intensified form which means to gaze, to be firmly fixed, to look steadily, or to look intently. This allows us to presume that Lot's wife stayed somewhere in the plain while she was firmly fixed. Another way to put it is...she was consumed with turning back, which was precisely what the Lord had told her *not to do*! The Lord said do not stay in the plain.

If she was looking back, it was physically impossible for her to see what was straight ahead! What distracted Lot's wife so much that she allowed herself to get caught up in the consumption? Was she concerned about her future sons-in-law? Maybe she was worried about other relatives or friends that were left behind; or was she afraid to leave what was familiar and step into the unknown? We just do not know. But, it draws upon a lesson of caution, that when we get distracted our chances of mishap significantly increase and then if we live through it, we must confront the consequences of disobedience. The result of Lot's wife's disobedience did not just impact her; it impacted her entire family. We discover at the end of this narrative that when Lot and his two daughters made it safely to Zoar, their new home, Lot had no wife for pro-creation. His two daughters felt compelled to step in as his 'wife' to multiply the land. This is not what God had purposed when he promised that they would multiply. Yet, God in his mercy forgave them.

Disobedience is usually undesirable. When I was a chaplain at a tier-one trauma center, I regularly witnessed the consequences of disobedience. I remember the thirty year old man who was rushed to the ER after a truck crashed into his motorcycle. He could hardly speak. His wife and young son were at his bedside and I asked him if he wanted me to pray. It was difficult for him to get the words out because of his pain, but he said yes, and said softly that he should have been more careful changing between lanes. The truck never saw him coming. Sadly, this young married man and father would be paralyzed for the rest of his life. Like Lot's wife, this man's disobedience would affect his family who would also pay the cost of his disobedience. Disobedience can be ugly. Lot's wife let her fears and distractions turn into disobedience. Distractions can significantly increase your chance of mishap or death. It can cause you to stumble, to fall, to become a pillar of salt…stuck in time…stuck in the past.

Another time I witnessed the negligence of a family member who paid more attention to the party she was attending and not enough to her two year old cousin whom she was babysitting. While she was preoccupied, the front door was open and the toddler walked out into a very busy main street. A truck hit the child, and the child died instantly. The parents were at work and rushed to the hospital without knowledge of their baby's condition. This was indeed one of my most difficult encounters as a chaplain. I had to be present with the doctor when he informed them that their baby was dead. I knew it was going to be a very long night, not just for me, and for the family, but for the doctor and nurses who were emotionally distraught. They restrained their emotions in front of the families, but I was trained to know when the staff might be disturbed or upset. You might be thinking that when one works in the ER, it must be something to get used to. Well, not so with children. This trauma center was not a children's hospital unit. Children rarely came to this ER. So when a tragedy like this occurs to a little baby, it can take one's breath away. It did for many of us that night.

My role as a chaplain is to be the anchor, the comforter and counselor to both staff and family. I was only able to do it by leaning on the strength of my Lord. The family was grieving and blaming one another while at the bedside of the baby. What made this so emotionally painful for the parents was that their baby was the same age as the cousin's toddler who was at the party with the baby that wandered outdoors. The parents could not understand how this cousin could watch her child and forget about the other. Sitting right next to each other in the ER, she could only reply "I'm sorry." She was also in pain and would have to deal with herself, and eventually forgive herself. The amazing grace was that even in death this baby was physically preserved and looking beautiful, like an angel. The only outward evidence of injury was the back of the baby's skull which the family never saw, thankfully due to the head bandage. They would be able to remember this baby in a good way. They would need at least that.

I stayed with this family for four hours until about two in the morning. The ministry I provided was only accomplished with the Holy Spirit guiding my every word and movement. There were long moments of complete silence, there was prayer, and in-between came outbursts of despair and crying. I did all that the Lord desired of me on that unforgettable night. I was willing to do whatever it was in letting grief have its way. For the blame, the pain and the anger would continue well beyond the walls of the ER and the wounds of disobedience would take many years to heal. A chaplain does not ever get to know what happens to the family after their time on the hospital unit. When they leave the unit that is it. I left them in God's care. God, the Master Maker over life and death, over our past and over our future. I can say that now with confidence!

CHAPTER TWO

NO PLACE LIKE HOME

If the home is deserving, let your peace rest on it;
if it is not, let your peace return to you.

—Matthew 10:13

There was literally no place like my home. Home for me was always changing but always the same. There were five constant companions that traveled with us…chaos, fear, alcohol, abandonment, and anger. No matter what kind of structure we lived in, three-family brownstone, two-family stucco, or a single-family clapboard ranch, the foundation of our home was built upon these five home-wreckers. When our home was destroyed by the fire, we stayed with relatives until my mother found an apartment. It was actually nicer and bigger than the other one and just two streets away, so I was able to be in a familiar neighborhood. The word familiar is an understatement. We moved from home to home as long as I can remember and we weren't even a military family.

One day my father came home very excited with *good news*. He told my mother that we were going to live in our own house. We were moving to the suburbs. I was five years old and really did not know what all of this meant. What I did know was that there was always some kind of big change happening in our lives, usually involving an unhappy ending. I guess I should have been happy. There would be no more busy city streets; we would live in our own house with a backyard. My dad also said that we might be able to get a puppy. Even with this prospect, I was not jumping for joy…and I was not alone. My sister Denise, who was ten years older than me, and my brother Tony, eight years older, were upset that they were moving from the city. They liked their schools, their childhood friends, and absolutely had no desire to relocate to the suburbs where racism was rampant. For them it was scary. For my three-year old brother Randy, he was clueless, as for me, I was indifferent.

This would be the second home that my father owned. The first home mortgage was secured by the federal home and edu-cational loan benefit from The Servicemen's Readjustment Act of 1944, a.k.a. G.I. Bill of Rights. The home was a beautiful three family with apple and cherry blossom trees. My dad's parents lived on the second floor. My auntie lived on the third floor with her children, and we were on the first floor. One year the government forced several home owners on this street in Roxbury to sell their homes to the government. The alternative meant they would lose their home. The reason for this push was because of a municipal project, a project that would not come to fruition until another twenty years. However, the money from this house sale afforded my dad the down payment for the new home in the 'burbs'.

Our move to the 'burbs' was unconventional to say the least. The company my father had been with was now relocating to

New Hampshire; employees had the option to relocate or lose their job. My father opted to find another job. Opportunities for black males were scarce. It was right before we moved that my dad secured a position as an insurance sale representative. Sales were far and few between, and the mortgage was soon in jeopardy. My father did not have a saving mentality, so gambling was usually his backup plan. If he did get a paycheck, a small bit went to food and bills, and a big chunk went to the dog track.

Guilt and regret tend to fuel the cycle of addiction. My father gambled big to make a lot of money, and then when he lost, the only way to live with the guilt was to try to fix it. Fix it meant to gamble again to recoup what he lost. The financial burden was exorbitant. The betting losses always, always, always outweighed the wins…in both frequency and dollar amount. His wins would never catch up. A gambling addict does not see gambling as the problem. The only problem for a gambling addict is losing, and the only solution is winning. This logic dictates that the only way to winning is by betting.

When I was an adult, my dad would occasionally make bitter statements about the injustices of this country…about the mistreatment of black Americans who built and fought for this country. There were accomplishments that he felt he could not be proud of, even when he should have. He had been an army World War II Veteran, yet, like most black vets, he was never allowed to hold a weapon for battle. His call of duty was to assist with medical errands or menial kitchen labor, and unlike the white vets who had returned from war as glorious heroes, my father, because of the color of his skin returned an invisible soldier. My father was denied other opportunities as well. His bitterness may have provided him the justification he needed to "to hit it big at the tracks" so he could 'fix everything' and make everything better for his wife and children.

Unfortunately, my entire family paid the cost for my father's financial recklessness. Add alcohol to this equation and the sum equals chaos. Dysfunction was at its all-time high. Promises whether big or small, were meant to be broken. This was the only plausible definition available to me as a child. A few broken promises can be overlooked. A lifestyle of broken promises become nothing but lies. Lies become the breeding ground for distrust. Though it was not their intention, my mother and father taught me how to not trust. These lessons of mistrust deepened the year we moved to our new house in the burbs. My father came home happily intoxicated one day and said that we were moving to the suburbs. A mere two years later, he told us that we're moving back to the city. So much happened during that time that it is difficult to chronicle the events. The good, the bad, the happy, the sad…are all jumbled together. I do happily recall that we got an adorable puppy from our neighbor's litter and named him Hobo. Hobo was the bright spot in our lives.

Money was getting tighter and tighter and the arguing between my mother and father became incessant. My dad drank more and my mother soon followed his lead. My sister and older brother experienced horrible isolation and discrimination at their predominantly white high school. The very first day of school my sister was shoved into a locker. They also experienced the word nigger for the first time. My mother taught us that this word was offensive and abusive, used to humiliate and to instill fear. Back then it was not expressed by blacks as a slang vernacular to be used as common everyday language between black and black. (I have also instructed my children to never use that word…ever). We can never forget our history…the days of slavery and Jim Crow. We can never use that word loosely or make jokes about it. We can never dismiss the pain, torture and death associated with that word which was, and is used as a weapon of hatred.

In the midst of this hatred and discrimination God delivered love to our family, and it was right next door. Our neighbors the Vechios were a white family that sincerely cared about us. I remember their chubby son who could not wait for me and my brother Randall to come out and play. The Vechios were indeed there for us. It is amazing how God always places the right people at the right time, to cross your path. You may recall the famous movie quote, "Show Me the Money!" Well, it became our family theme. There were days when we had absolutely no money. No money in the penny jar, no money in any pockets, no money between the sofa cushions, no money anywhere. Bills were not met. A few times, our electricity or gas would be disconnected. The worst was when we had no food. My mother was a fantastic cook and knew how to make food stretch. If there were such a thing, she could make stone soup appetizing. But zero plus zero equals zero. When there was absolutely nothing in the kitchen cabinets or in the fridge, my mother would suck up her pride and ask Mrs. Vechio for money so we could eat. If my dad was not home to drive my mother, Mrs. Vechio would gladly drive her to the grocery store. When our electricity was turned off, the Vechios loaned us money to have it reconnected. Even when Mr. Vechio was shot to death while helping a friend in Roxbury, Mrs. Vechio continued to be loving and gracious to our family. She was never condescending and helped us with a cheerful heart. I believe she thought that my mother was already embarrassed and depressed. Mrs. Vechio would have been correct in her thinking. My mother never liked to be in desperate situations as it exposed my father's incapacity to care for his own family. It presented black people in a negative light living up to the stereotypes that blacks are lazy and irresponsible. I can only imagine the anguish and humiliation of my mother being trapped, isolated and betrayed…trapped, because she was dependent on others to do even the smallest errands, having no license. She was isolated, because her best friends lived in the city; friends she had known most of her life. Betrayed, because her husband, who she promised to be with until death do them part, was not the responsible man she had wed. Sometime during that year, her drinking became self-indulgent. Prior to this move, my mother had always been a light social drinker with an occasional drink or two when they played bid whist with their couple of friends or when they went out for an evening of dinner and dancing. Her moods started to swing for the worse.

In the beginning she had made every attempt to hide her tears from us, but with her increased drinking, she no longer hid her hurt and desperately wanted someone's pity, even if it had to be her children. There is a very big danger in drinking alone and drinking in despair. It is a downer and has great power in making your already dark world, darker. My mother saw no glimpse of light at the end of a very long and dark tunnel. Substance abuse of any kind is the perpetual engine that sustains the never-ending cycle of despair. It creates the false truth that there will be no daybreak, there will be no sunshine. I believe that is what my mother thought that late night when I found her sitting on a chair in front of the oven with her head inside. It must have been a weekend, because that was when my father stayed out with his gambling and drinking buddies. I walked into the kitchen very puzzled. I told her I was thirsty and asked, "Mommy what are you doing in the oven and what is that funny smell? She was crying and said she was tired. She got me water, brought me back to bed and tucked me in. I went right to sleep. I did not realize what she was doing until several years later when I caught her again…trying to end her life the same way, by turning on a burner that didn't light and hoping that the fumes would kill her. Her sadness, hurt and bitterness had become part of my persona. I don't know how close that incident was to the day she got notice of our foreclosure and the day we moved back to the city, back to Roxbury. I don't know if we lived in the suburb of Rockland a full year. We were the only black family in our neighborhood. It was a negative reflection on the whole concept of blacks moving into white suburbia. Most of the whites did not want us there from the start. That was indicative when the neighborhood conducted a meeting about a black family (us) moving in. I'm sure it was a great day in the neighborhood when our moving truck moved us back to the city "where we belong". For my older siblings it was also a great day because they could get back in a safe and comfortable routine with real friends again. For my little brother, he was still young and clueless. For me, it was not a great day because it was something different again. I decided that day, that change was not good. When change happens things got worse.

During these years my mother tried to help and protect my father's reputation the best way she knew how. Today, we call it enabling. About six months after my father returned to the city he was hired by a major electric company that also made airplane turbine engines. He went to work from 8 am. to 5 pm as an assembly worker, rarely tardy and rarely absent. He got promotions over the years, but it did not matter since the dog track got most of his salary. Whatever my mother could secure for work she took it, part-time or full-time. For a period, she had also been a part-time church secretary. For my mother, it was always just trying to stay barely above water. That was the gist of her adult life. She worked hard and was usually stressed. She once said that she never had anything to show for her work and would have many sleepless nights of worry. My mother was frugal counting every penny just so we could survive week to week. I do not remember my mother ever taking a vacation since her honeymoon. She tried to protect and care for us the best she knew how. On several Christmas occasions, she would get a ride from one of her friends to buy our gifts the night before. Christmas holidays were never extravagant and always stressful. I actually believed in Santa Clause until one year I saw my mother putting just a few presents under the tree, basically one gift per child. Tears dropped from her cheeks. My mother wanted to do more for us. It was that night that I no longer respected the notion of a Santa Claus. It was my mother's hard work and tears that put gifts under the tree, not some white fairy tale character that took all the credit for her love and diligence.

Of course, we celebrated December 25th as the birth of Jesus with card exchanges, the angel at the top of the tree, and dinner at my father's parent's house. Pretty much that was it. We did not go to church as a family unless it was a wedding or funeral occasion. Church had once been a major part of my parent's lives. My parents grew up Episcopalian. My father went to church as a young boy and his parents had a big picture of the Last Supper in their dining room. In a way, it mesmerized me. My maternal grandmother was a devout Christian. She volunteered in many church capacities. She played the hymns on the piano in their parlor and took her six children to Sunday service; her youngest son was an altar boy. My parent's Christian upbringing spilled over into our lives when we were young children. My mother almost always tucked us in bed and then had us recite the goodnight prayer, "Now I lay me down to sleep, I pray the Lord my soul to keep, if I should die before I wake, I pray my Lord, my soul to take." I remember the framed image of Jesus between the photos of Martin Luther King Jr. and President John F. Kennedy which hung proudly in our living room. I wish my parents had stayed committed to the Lord because I believe their marriage would have been different. I believe my childhood would have been different.

My parents succumbed to their distractions of money problems, drinking problems, racial problems, and family problems. They unconsciously rearranged their priorities placing God last.

When my dad lost his bets, he drank more. When he drank, he either got loud and/or mean. He never hit my mother, but his tone of voice and his yelling always frightened us. Sometimes he would enter our home late at night talking loudly, then ultimately yelling at my mother when she would tell him to quiet down because the children are sleeping. As my mother's alcohol intake increased, she too, became a yeller. Soon there were many sleepless nights with both of them yelling. The arguments were about the same stuff…bills, clothes for the kids, food for school lunch, and on and on and on. It was a living hell. Yet, in spite of these nightmarish events, life went on.

After the fire, when we finally settled into our bigger apartment, it seemed like normalcy might enter my world. I was in the second grade trying to make friends. Randy was in kindergarten trying to adjust to the concept of school. My sister Denise was in her last year of high school preparing for college; she kept an average of A's and A+'s. She was like my second mother taking care of me and my younger brother. She loved the music of Motown and whenever she could save a few dollars she would buy 45 records and invite her friends over. That's how I learned the words to the songs from those much older than my generation. My brother Tony was the star basketball athlete making news in the city sport pages. Tony had a fantastic personality and was well-liked by his teachers, coaches and peers. He was kind, fun- loving, studied hard managing a B+ average. Both of them worked part-time jobs while in high school; they had to if they wanted clothes, lunch money and spending money as they could not depend on my father for anything, including tuition. Both would obtain college grants and scholarships; it was a given that they would work while in college. I admired both of them and looked up to them as role models. Predictably, I would follow their lead. I studied hard like Denise, and played basketball hard like Tony. I even secured his number 15 for my high-school basketball t-shirt; of course I played the position of guard!

Normalcy was again interrupted. Enter drama. It was the first week of summer and very early in the morning. I was almost eight years old and entering third grade in the fall. My mother woke me first and told me to quickly get dressed. While I did as she said, she got Randall ready. I asked her, "Why did we have to get up so early when school was out, and where are we going?" She hastily replied, "We're moving without your father." Then she demanded, "No more questions." My mother had our suitcases as full as she could and we took the few toys we possessed. She collected the family photos and albums. That was about it. One of my older cousins drove us plus Hobo to my mother's brother's ex-wife's apartment around the corner from The Boston Symphony Hall in Back Bay. Tony and Denise met us there later that evening.

It may have only been about three miles from where we lived in Roxbury, but our move to Back Bay was a move to another dark place in my young life. My mother's independence would not be easy, resulting in a four month stay with her ex-sister-in-law. My aunt Carmen was a single mother raising two teen sons. I actually enjoyed this company. She was the epitome of patience and kindness. A great benefit to us was her Puerto Rican heritage, a culture of spicy food and spicy music. Her dialect was just as enjoyable, especially when she exaggerated, to teach us a few words and phrases. A devout Catholic, she loved the Lord, loved all people, and loved family. She loved my mother dearly. My aunt Carmen was a sunflower, a burst of brightness that shone before the next storm.

Initially, there was no great love loss being separated from my father. At first, this move was refreshing. My mother was working full-time as an executive secretary for a blood research laboratory institute. She was a proficient typist at 125 words per minute. It was back-in-the-day before computers and electronic delete buttons existed. My mother was intelligent and industrious. She was one of only two Black employees, and was quickly noticed for her professionalism and integrity. She had opportunities to fly around the world as an executive assistant, but declined due to her fear of flying. She enjoyed her job and enjoyed having her own apartment; everything seemed to be going well but I soon discovered that her happiness was temporary as my mother was lonely and very bitter towards my father. The way she paid him back was by not allowing us to visit him or his family, and the reality was that it also punished us. We missed them all, our grandparents, cousins, uncles and aunts. My mother's sadness and bitterness kept her committed to the bottle, making her sadder and more bitter.

I understood that my father never gave child support or helped my mother in any way as she struggled financially to keep us above water. We were well-aware that our parents were not good together, yet we were children and missed our father. My mother used us as weapons against my father and told us everything bad about him and then for the sake of her pride and pain, she sacrificed our connection to our father and to his family. Every once in a while he would come by to see us and would buy ice cream for me, Randy and for any friends that were with us. His visits were always brief and always ended in arguments with my mother. It was about this time when I stopped calling her mommy and used the term "Ma", which is what my older siblings called her. Maybe I did this as a way to try to grow up fast and be done with that kid stuff. It was becoming too messy and too confusing.

When she didn't drink and was not drowning in self-pity, our home was a great place to be. She loved all kinds of music ranging from classical to Nat King Cole. She was also a great dancer in pointe ballet, modern jazz and tap. This had been her dream… to dance. In her teens she was a dancer in the Negro Ensemble

Troupe of Roxbury. Ma loved taking us to the POPS summer concerts at the half-shell on the Charles River, and she also took us to the Boston Commons "frog pond" and to historical walks in downtown Boston. Whenever she could get discount tickets to the science and art museums we excitedly packed bag lunches anticipating a day of creative fun. A few times my mother set up weekend trips for me and Randy to visit her brother and his family in the suburbs. We actually loved going, especially in the summer! My uncle was so much fun; he would pick us up and bring us to his home and entertain us by pretending to have a voice like Donald Duck and tell us stories. They also had an above-ground pool and a huge backyard! It seemed huge to us. We played all day with our cousins and in the evening my auntie played her favorite hymns on their upright piano. As usual, we came home happy and ready to see ma and Tony. Denise was away attending her first year at college.

This return home from my uncle's was very different; my uncle was very quiet and looked like he was about to cry. When we entered our home, a detective was in our living room. Our good neighbor and dear friend to my mother, was by her side. Ma was holding back her tears. Tony was in his room. Our neighbor explained to me and Randall, that a bad man had hurt our mother. The intruder entered through my bedroom window which was accessible by the alley fire escape as apparently the window lock did not secure completely. The intruder entered in the dark without making hardly any noise, and carefully pushed my hamster cage to the side so he could step on top of my bureau. The evidence was in plain view with his two big shoe prints on the bureau.

My mother had fallen asleep on the couch watching television with Hobo who was now older and much slower. Neither knew that this stranger was in our home until my mother awoke to his hand cupping her mouth. He had one knee on her chest while kicking Hobo with his other leg. He almost killed Hobo, and would have done more harm to her and to my mother if Tony had not been home. God's angels once again protected our family. Tony was supposed to work late that night. Instead, he came home early, and went to bed after some studying. While the intruder covered my mother's mouth, she mustered all the strength she could and bit his hand; her scream woke my brother who immediately rescued her and Hobo. Ma, Tony, and Hobo chased this intruder down our long hallway through our kitchen to the backdoor. My mother threw her big cast iron frying pan and hit the back of his head. The police said they did not have enough evidence to find this person, in spite of the fact that there had been recent similar home invasions like this in our neighborhood with robbery not as the motive. The motive was probably rape. Speculation by the neighborhood tenants was that he was also a serial killer and had been watching and casing apartments of single women in the neighborhood. In spite of the notion that the person was familiar with my mother's routine, and knew that we were gone, knew to move the cage on top of my bureau in the dark without a sound, and knew that the window was not secured, the police disregarded the evidence and dismissed the possibility of that speculation. My mother got a glimpse of the man who was maybe Black or Latino. The police stated that the perpetrator was most likely my mother's boyfriend or ex-husband. Ma was appalled. She knew my father would never do anything like that, and she knew it was not a boyfriend, because the man she was keeping company with was a white man. My mother got a glimpse of the intruder who was a man of color. Ma chalked it up to good ole fashion racism. She knew after a few days, the police department would put this aside…and that is what they did. They did not care that our family lived in fear every day wondering if the intruder would come back to finish what he started.

My mother went to work thinking everyday she might be followed and attacked. Our dog Hobo had been kicked in the stomach and was doing her best to hang on. For the next several weeks, Randall and I slept with my mother in her bed. I would only go into my bedroom during the day. I could not get the image of the intruder's shoe marks out of my head and my dreams kept turning into nightmares. Tony kept cool on the outside being the man of the house, but I knew he was just as shaken and disturbed as we were. We were all scared and scarred by this experience and we wanted so badly to get out of that apartment. My mother was trying hard to find us another apartment and in a few more weeks, she did. We were happy and sad. It meant we would be out of that apartment but it also meant that we would be going to another neighborhood and making friends all over again. As always, my mother tried to make the best of our situation. She said this would be better for us and we'd do just fine. She told us, "Don't worry about that intruder, he won't follow us here." She then said with a chuckle, "If they ever find that man, he will have a gigantic lump on the back of his head. As hard as I hit him, he ought to have that lump for life."

As positive as I tried to be then, the past events and the past years tainted my world view. Just when I thought bad things would never happen again to our family, tragedy would occur. I equated moving with tragedy. I began to despise change, developing a defense against the future.

CHAPTER THREE

AFRAID OF THE UNKNOWN

For God did not give us a spirit of timidity,
but a spirit of power, of love and of self-discipline.

—2 TIMOTHY 1:7

Lot's wife might have paused in the past because she was afraid to go forward, afraid of the unknown, afraid of the unfamiliar. I can relate to this fear of the future. I lived in a dysfunctional household in which the unknown and the unfamiliar had become the norm. By the way, I never knew my home was labeled 'dysfunctional'. I was not privy to that term until college. I grew up in a city neighborhood where most of us lived with some of the same issues so it was 'normal' and 'regular' to us. Inconsistency had become consistent. Though in no way does this imply I was used to that lifestyle, what it does mean is that I developed a set of coping skills—some were good and some, not so good. Essentially those were my survival tools.

The pursuit of education was one of my positive coping skills. Studying hard, getting good grades in school and the sense of achievement distracted me from the chaos at home. I credit my mother for instilling education into my head when I was very young. She always made me feel proud whenever I brought my report card home with A's and B's. I enjoyed this flirtation with good grades until it came to a halt in the third grade. I looked at my report card and there it was, a C next to mathematics. I cried all the way home. That C had betrayed me and now I would betray my hard working mother. I was upset and full of anxiety that I would disappoint her. To my surprise, Ma assured me that it was not the end of the world and said that all she wanted from her children was for them to do their best. She said if I did my best then a C was okay with her. I did feel a bit better not disappointing her, but I still believed I was a failure to myself. I was now determined more than ever to know all of the multiplication table and rid myself of the scarlet letter 'C'. Mission accomplished…until the seventh grade.

Up to this point I had teachers that wanted their students to learn, wanted their students to understand, and to enjoy math. But this teacher, Sister Agnes, found more joy in making the math problem more difficult than it was. The ones that managed to succeed in spite of her methods received her public praise. She made math to be a mystery that could only be unlocked by the privileged few and highly exceptional. Good grades were never easy for me; I had to study long and hard to manage a B average with a few occasional A's. Seventh grade math took me to a whole new level of academic frustration. It did not help that I was petrified to ask clarifying questions in class, which only worsened my predicament. Sister Agnes seemed like it was her mission in life to call students to the chalk board to solve math problems. I hated and feared being called out. I knew that I did not know how or where to begin and felt naked in front of the class. Math had become a foreign language to me. No matter how hard I studied, I could not understand the concepts. I could not make the connections on my own. When I built up the courage in private to ask her for help, she responded in a condescending manner, magnifying my embarrassment and sense of failure. This was the same teacher that out of the blue had everyone line up around the room and asked a white female student to stand in the middle. This student had two perfect braids with white ribbons on each end. Her plaid parochial uniform had pleats that could stand up to a hurricane, and her white Peter Pan collar was as white as a first snow fall. Her black and white saddle shoes had not a single scuff mark. Sister Agnes said, "Now class, this how you should wear your uniform; this is how you should come to school every day." 99 per cent of the white students wore their uniforms as exemplified by "Polly Perfect", the teacher's pet student, who basked in her 15 minutes of fame.

Indeed, this was a classist and racist moment for the rest of us, the one per cent comprised mostly of poor Black students. Besides me, the rest of the Black female students did not have long straight hair to fashion into two long braids. Our parents could not afford to dry clean our uniforms. Most of us got surplus uniforms that the school had for charity given by other graduated students. Already embarrassed by wearing used clothing, I was now put on display again. My used school shirts had a grey tint from being washed and bleached so many times. My mother could barely afford my one pair of brown and tan saddle shoes. Until that moment, I had actually liked those saddle shoes, but now like everything else, I was told that my clothes and physical presentation were not good enough.

Enough was enough for us black students, so we decided to show off our cultural pride and wear as much red, black and green as we could. These were the colors of the late sixties and seventies reflecting a pride in our African and Black heritage. The red signified the bloodshed of our ancestors, green identified the Mother Land, Africa, and black represented the color of our race. In our way it was a small revolution; we wore ribbons, socks, sweaters anything red, black or green. It was a brief revolt that ended a week later when the teaching nuns and administration threatened anyone who wore colors other than red, white and blue, with suspension. I certainly could not afford missed school days with the real war I was already having with math.

Unfortunately, my math did not improve. Fear evolved to terror at the thought of going to the chalkboard. I developed a mental block. Even when I thought the answer was correct, I second guessed myself and went with the incorrect solution. It would be years later before I even wanted to make attempts at understanding math which had become my nemesis. I resolved to hone in on my likes, my strengths which were blossoming in history, writing and poetry.

Boston was conducting a citywide essay contest. I thought about submitting an essay, but did not have the confidence. I mentioned the notion to my mother who encouraged and pumped me up so much, I knew I could win. I needed this esteem booster. When I told it to Sister Agnes, who was also my homeroom and English teacher, she strongly advised me that I should wait until next year. I told her I did not want to wait and that I had already selected my historical heroine...Marian Anderson. She was a hero to me for being the first black opera singer to perform at Carnegie Hall. In the midst of racism, poverty and hardship she pursued her singing dream. She was a fighter; she was determined. I think that is what drew me to her as a subject. Sister Agnes said that Anderson was not a historical hero. I fought back with persistence, telling her that Anderson was a hero. I was passionate about this essay and nothing or no one would get in the way of this mission… not even Sis. Agnes.

In spite of her discouraging words and lack of support in my preparation, my essay was submitted. I won first place in the seventh grade category! The ceremony was at Copley's Boston Public Library, Boston's biggest and oldest library, with the Mayor giving each winner a handshake and certificate. I was elated. I think I surprised myself. It was as if I had won a million dollars. But it was far more than what money could buy. It was the fact that I was smart enough, diligent enough, and creative enough to actually win. I was victor over the racism and bigotry of Sis. Agnes. For a brief minute, I was victor over my low self-worth, and Ma was right there to witness my victory. I knew what it meant for my mother to take time off from work. It meant she took public transportation to see me, public transportation back to work, and then she would work late to make up the lost time. She would return home tired and still have to prepare dinner, review our homework and make lunches for the next day. I never took that for granted. It meant the world to me to see her smile as I received the certificate, which I still have. Her eyes were saying, I knew you could do it. It was nice to watch her enjoy the here and now, even if it had been for but a brief moment. As for me, it was a respite for me to bask in the present moment. I did not think about the past or the future.

Whenever I prepared for a scholastic project, I would totally immerse myself, which allowed me to tune out the chaos at home and focus on my achievement. Since ma and dad separated, my mother's bitterness festered like a quake with minor shakes leading up to the full quake, then leaving the residual of the aftershock. She was angry at my dad for not contributing financially, and not being able to rely on him for any support. Ma worked so hard, sometimes taking on one or two part-time jobs on top of her full-time secretarial position. She even donated her blood for a small amount of money to help pay for groceries or to reconnect the electricity and gas. She would come home exhausted after work, cook dinner, make our lunches and get us ready for school. She did nothing to pamper herself. I think that is why I helped her with the housework in addition to our regular chores. My sister was in college and my brothers were either too busy to help or oblivious to the dirt. At the age of ten, I was beginning to grow up fast.

In addition to my mother being bitter and exhausted rearing four children single-handedly, my mother was lonely for a male companion, someone to hold her, someone to listen to her pain, someone to tell her she was still attractive, and someone to tell her that she was loved. These are things she said to me as a young girl who did not fully comprehend this need even when she tried to fulfil that need. I saw Ma take chances on men; men who never gave and always took advantage of her desperation and vulnerability. She was attracted to men who made promises then quickly broke them. She was attracted to men who were alcoholics. It was a comfortable affinity.

There is nothing deep or profound about the obvious pattern in my mothers' selection of male companionship. She did not think enough of herself to set higher standards, so she settled for much less. She settled for what she thought was comfortable. Sadly, the men in my mother's lives did nothing to better her lifestyle. There was one incident when her boyfriend came by to bring us to his place for the weekend. Ma had been seeing him for a few months. That night Randy and I awoke to them arguing. They had been drinking and his voice was becoming more aggressive. He frightened us. I really thought that he slapped Ma, but when I asked her she said no. We took a cab home that night. I was only eleven then and told her that if he calls or comes by the house, I would call the police. I also told my big brother Tony what happened. My mother soon realized that her beau was not worth putting herself or her kids in harm's way. I was glad to see him no more, but my mother drank more to compensate for her 'loneliness'. She grew more impatient with us and was now more 'tired'. Her complaining and bitterness was at times overwhelming for me.

By the time I was in eighth grade, I started to stay away from home as long as I could. I would do homework over at my friends' house and then play basketball with the guys in our hood who were twelve to twenty-one years old. Four of us girls played well enough to compete and handle the pressure. We were either respected or hated for playing basketball 'on their court'. Sometimes if you out-played a dude he would push or shove an elbow at you. Honestly it did not matter, as long as my hook shot went in or my pass was complete. Playing basketball was my retreat, and like my academics, I practiced every day to get better and to be able to hang with the guys on the court. It was a bragging accomplishment especially the weekend my brother Tony came home from college. He decided to play and I was on his team. It was so cool because the big talk-ers had no idea that my brother was a talented player. My mother had taught Tony a few ballet tricks so he could move with more agility. Watching him arch and shoot was a pretty sight and when he moved he was quick and smooth, gliding on the court. It was amazing how high he could jump for a short player.

Tony was serious about his craft and at the same time he had fun playing. He received a partial basketball college scholarship and when the money was exhausted, his part time job could not afford the cost. He then had to transfer to a state college. It broke his heart that he was not on a team playing basketball. Basketball had been Tony's escape. He decided to major in social service and was drawn to helping troubled teen boys. He managed to volunteer as a mentor while working and studying. Whenever Tony came to visit, he brought nothing but sunshine and laughter. He and his friends were funny crazy. They sang to 'Earth, Wind and Fire' and schooled me and Randall on the new dances. Tony even let me visit a weekend with his girlfriend Mandy. This was the same girl who was his high school sweetheart. I was fifteen and thought that college was cool. Three of Tony's college friends had also gone to high school with him. They were grounded and smart. Tony kept good company.

Tony's visits home started to become more frequent. He was solo, no friends, no Mandy. He told Ma that he broke up with Mandy. He started to have random discussions about his world view, about life. Up to this point, I never saw Tony with any kind of drug. He never even smoked cigarettes. But now he was keeping himself in his room smoking marijuana. My mother told him this was not allowed. He knew that, but continued. Prior to this, I never saw Tony disrespect my mother. I guess he began losing respect with her increased drinking. I had had it also. One day afterschool I hid her gin bottle. After dinner she was ready to watch TV and looked in the bottom cabinet for her drug and it was not there. She started yelling, "Who moved my alcohol?" She ranted for few more minutes until I could not take anymore. I fessed up. I told her she didn't need it; it only makes her sad or angry. She glared at me and with slow calculated syllables she said, "Doooon't ever mooove my gin again." I never did.

Tony returned to school on Sunday. That Friday he came home and informed us that he was not going back to college. Tony was a great student, great brother, and great human being. As I write this, I cannot resist the tears as I think of how he had just one semester left until his graduation. I remember how proud he was with his super wide smile the day he graduated from high school. He would never graduate again. We would never see that smile again.

My mother and Denise tried to find out what was going on with Tony. They could not get a straight answer from his best buddies or his ex-girlfriend. There was a rumor that Tony unknowingly had been given the drug Phencyclidine (PCP) also known as Angel Dust, and he "started to trip". If this was the case, the word trip does not come close to what I witnessed. Tony spiraled into an existence of evil and darkness. I was in the tenth grade during this craziness. I was trying so hard to do well in school. This was not any school; I had received full scholarship to Commonwealth School, one of Boston's oldest and esteemed private high schools.

The days were good for me. I was busy with classes, basketball practice and games. I was excited to have made the team as starting guard. I had to take a subway train to and from school and got anxiety returning home every day. I never looked forward to getting off the train because it meant I would soon be home. I could not anticipate what kind of evening would greet me at the door. Would it be my mother drunk and depressed or drunk and angry? Would it be Tony talking weird while sitting in the dark? It made me feel scared and unsettled. His personality was altered. He no longer laughed or smiled. He demanded that Randall, who was only thirteen, get marijuana for him on the dangerous section of drug infested, Blue Hill Avenue or get it from some of the most dangerous housing projects in the city. He secretly threatened Randall that he would beat him if he told Ma. Tony had no desire to play basketball except for twirling the basketball on one finger and saying he was earth, wind and fire. He shaved his head completely.

He would sit in the family room for hours sitting in the dark and staring at the blank television screen. His other past time was to go upstairs to his room and smoke marijuana. One night in his usual position staring at the blank television in the dark, he got up and walked erratically around the room mumbling unidentifiable words. He looked at me and said nothing. I left the room because the look was horrific. All I remember are the whites of his eyes glaring at me. I went to my room crying and told my mother how

I could not take any more of this. When she confronted Tony he yelled at her saying that she was the reason our family broke up, she was the reason dad was not here and she was the reason everything was messed up. He started to approach my mother; Randy was next to her. I yelled at Tony and told him to get away from Ma. He turned to me, his eyes glaring and put his hands around my throat. It was as if Tony was gone and this evil spirit was instead residing within him. Ma and Randy got him off of me, then I ran outside. Ma called the state mental institution that was around the corner from our three-family house and they came and took Tony away. We all cried. It was devastating.

My mother had to do what she knew to do and that was to protect us. The plethora of drug addiction and mental resources that exist today were not readily accessible back in those days. The very next day we went to visit Tony, but they would not allow us to be with him. They said it was too soon. We were able to visit him within the next few days and it was sad because Tony was like a zombie. He just sat in front of a window looking out. He said nothing, hardly acknowledging us. Ma decided that we would back off for a while. It was too difficult for us and I felt guilt for him being there. I had thought that if I did not tell my mother how much Tony freaked me out, she would not have said anything to him and he would not have gotten upset. The reality is that at some point Tony was going to break no matter what.

We visited a few weeks later; Tony smiled. His hair was growing back. He did not say much but he was glad to see us. We each hugged him. We were no longer afraid of him but we felt sorry for him. The hospital psychiatrists could not tell us much other than what we already knew, that Tony had had a 'mental breakdown' and was in a psychosis state. Their solution in spite of an undetermined diagnosis was to keep him sedated or 'calm'. Tony was institutionalized for almost eight months. He was never the same.

He did not express extreme emotions; he was never jovial, violently angry or weeping sad. Our family grew extremely suspect of his institution. We had often wondered if he had received shock therapy. Shock therapy was common, but not widely accepted, yet it was quietly practiced through the mid-seventies. Since it was not an illegal procedure, there was no real case to pursue. When my mother confronted them about their over-medication and possible shock therapy, the doctors and administration provided a professional response implying that their procedures were justifiable because of Tony's (one and only) violent episode. She was a poor black single woman making an attempt to wake up this systemic sleeping giant. She would not have had substantial legal grounds against the hospital since she voluntarily committed her son. She would have been crushed by its bureaucracy.

While going through life's ordeals I never took time to assess the long-term detriments. I only knew what I needed for that particular time to get me through my brother's and mother's conditions. I stuck it out at Commonwealth as long as I could. It was the middle of my junior year when I met with the School Master, Mr. Charles E. Merrill and told him what was happening in my household. I told him that I could not stand up to the academic pressure at Commonwealth under those conditions, and that I would be leaving after Christmas break.

A gracious and sensitive man, Mr. Merrill encouraged me to stay, and offered to provide me the extra support necessary to maintain my grades. A part of me wanted badly to accept his offer; the other part of me was just tired. I was tired of everything… my brother's psychosis, my mother's drinking, her bitterness, her anger, and yelling. I was tired of being ashamed of my life and my family. All of it, including the academic pressure, was a ton of bricks crushing down on the top of my head. I told Mr. Merrill that I needed a break. I did not know what that meant or what I was going to do next. He hugged me and said he understood and respected my decision to withdraw and assured me that when I submitted my college references I could use him as a reference and he would write recommendations for any of my college applications. Mr. Merrill would be good on his promise. He was a white man who did not care about my color, and only saw my potential. As soon as I left his office, I regretted my decision to quit, because I was again fearful of my future. I was giving up basketball, my school friends, and probably my academic future. I could have gone right back into his office and accepted his offer to stay, but instead, cleaned out my locker, left the building, and sobbed my way to the subway station.

All I could tell my mother was that it was too hard to focus at such a demanding school. I could not to tell her that it was because of her and Tony. When we love, we are not aware of the fine line of enabling someone to continue in their brokenness. I did not know any better. It broke her heart that I left Commonwealth, yet she hugged me and told me she understood. By the time Tony was released from the mental hospital, his medical status was mental disability. This allowed him subsidized housing. Tony was not able to organize his mind the way he could when he was in college. He mentioned a few times that he wanted to finish school, but he only grew frustrated with any attempt to concentrate for long periods. For about two years, he worked a few different part-time jobs, then one day Tony was gone. He left everything in his apartment. No one knew where he went, we did not know if he was alive or dead until a relative noticed him at my mother's funeral. He was not seen again until my wedding when a friend informed me that my brother Tony was outside the church. I was overjoyed to finally see him, but my friend said he left. It would be seven years before we heard from Tony. He wound up living in a nursing home in Fresno, California. The brother I once knew was no longer. It was another piece of my family system that was totally broken. I could only pick up the broken pieces in my life and continue in spite of my fears, in spite of the unknown and in spite of myself.

CHAPTER FOUR

LITTLE GIRL LOST

…that any of these little ones should be lost.

—Matthew 18:14

I was lost in many ways as a little girl. I was lost being the middle child. I was lost in the middle of constant familial dysfunction. I was lost in the middle of my race, as light skinned with long straight hair…and I was lost spiritually. I attribute this loss to a loss of connectivity and loss of identity. I had two older siblings, who for all the right reasons were not readily available. I had a younger brother who was the last born, and acted out our family dysfunction with his pursuit of being the center of positive or negative attention.

Lot's future sons-in-law might have taken for granted that they would have belonged to a complete family unit. When Lot spoke to them to get out of that place, they forsook Lot's leadership and forsook his guidance and protection as the patriarch.

They instead made a fatal choice of staying. I did not have the privilege of a patriarch to guide me to better places or to protect me from life's harm. I had my father's sir name, yet no father to call upon or to look up to, except for very rare drop-ins. I had a mother, who was too lost in her stuff to see that I was lost. A lack of identity puts you in limbo; you don't know who you really are, or to whom you really belong. Recently I heard on the radio, that light skinned women get easier breaks. I could not resist chuckling to myself and thinking that they should read my book because there was nothing easy about anything in my life. As I continued to listen, I thought about the difficult time I had growing up because some of my dark skinned sisters had thought exactly the same thing as this radio guest, and how they had rejected me because of the stereotype, even if the stereotype was false.

I was just six years old when I experienced my first intra-racist encounter. It was the first day of school (a school that was predominantly black). In spite of my introversion, I was actually happy and excited to attend school. I was ready to meet the world, even if it was only a few blocks away. My mother like most black mothers in the sixties' dressed their children the best that they could especially for the first few days of school. It meant having your hair done nicely and wearing a nice dress or skirt. I felt pretty, and even special, because I didn't often get to wear nice dresses. Pretty and nice soon came to a halt on my very first day of school. I was standing with the rest of the new first graders when a flying pigeon dropped its business on me. At first I had no idea what had landed on my head and then trickled onto my dress until another student laughed while pointing at me. Within seconds all the kids near me joined in this school yard activity of humiliation. It was bad enough being the center of attention and laughed at, but it became cruel when two dark skinned girls came over to me

40

laughing, and one said, "That's what you get for having long hair with your piss colored self." All I could is cry. I had no clue why I was being treated this way. I had just come from a predominantly white suburb and was trying to make sense as to why they hated me and my family, but having one of my own speak to my color was confusing, and a whole lot more painful. It was as if my long hair and light skin repelled them.

Maybe I was too close in skin color to white, reminding them of what the whites were doing to us colored Americans in own country and to our colored soldiers in Viet Nam who were being treated as if they were the enemy. Whatever the reason, I was too young and too ill-equipped to figure the why. Even in this emotional flux, I do not recall telling my mother. I wanted to, but there was always a grown up Dyanne inside of me ready to protect my mother from additional drama. Unfortunately, I continued dealing with my problem in this way by keeping painful experiences to myself, which only accentuated my introversion.

Although I was afraid of being rejected, I made attempts at making friends. I possessed a strong need to find a safe emotional place with people my age, with people my race. I was never concerned about their shade of black. So I continued to take chances; chances that seemed to emotionally set me back instead of moving me ahead.

School had become a not-so-friendly place for me; at least in the mental box I had placed it, right next to betrayal and rejection. I responded by being alone most of the time in and after school. It was my safe zone. One day I decided to step out of my safe zone. Excitement was in the air when a few kids in my neighborhood invited me to play with them. I was now in the second grade and was not often asked by other kids. Group dynamic theory dictates that in every group (no matter the age) there exists at least one person, who will emerge as the leader. In this group of boys and girls, a dark skinned girl smiled as she approached me and asked me if I wanted to play this new game called follow me. I shook my head yes, smiling. She said you have to close your eyes and do what I say. I walked in front of her as she guided me with her hand on my back, while the rest followed. I heard giggling. It was about a minute journey when she said, "Okay keep your eyes closed and bend down." After the word down, I was pushed. My eyes were now wide open as I landed on something that had a stench like none other. I was on top of a dead decomposing black cat. Its skeleton was partially exposed. Horrified.

A tear rolled down my cheek, but I was determined not let them see me cry. I felt that I could not expose my weakness. I just looked up at them as if to say why. Deep down I knew why. It was because of my complexion and hair length. It took me a minute to get up because I had to figure out how to stand up without touching the cat for the second time. When I was to my feet I walked out of their sight. Then I ran, crying, long and hard until I got home. Again, I don't recall telling my mother of this incident. I did not venture out much after that and stayed to myself in and out of school. My older sister had close friends, and their younger sisters would occasionally spend time with me. But it was not on regular basis; most of them were a year or two older than me. I no longer had the courage to initiate or trust friend-ships. Rejection was becoming my new friend. The next year was the year my mother had left my dad and moved us to Back Bay Boston. It was a neighborhood comprised of whites, blacks and Puerto Ricans. I chose to stay home after school rather than take chances on finding friends. Instead, a few kids who lived in the same building, found me.

It was pretty comforting to be part of a group of white and black girls. We were around the same age. My black friends enjoyed braiding my hair and the hair of the two white girls. It is how I first learned to cornrow braids. We had fun. Then it changed. Someone said we should go to the park at Fenway. What a sight to behold In the middle of the city with lots of grass and trees. The park had picnic tables and swing sets and a big rubber tire attached by two separate ropes which made it nice for two to swing together. We were about to swing on the tire with one of the other girls, when my dark skinned friend persuaded me to swing by myself. She told Liz, my Caucasian friend to push the tire. Instead of pushing, she twisted the swing. I got dizzy and the ropes became wrapped around my throat. These two were laughing hard, maybe not realizing how dangerous it was. I probably would have suffocated if one of the other girls had not stopped the tire.

I was again emotionally lost and confused. Was it my hair, my skin? Why was I always the one that stood out like a sore thumb? I went home never telling my mother what happened and asked her to cut my hair. I made up a story that I wanted a cut like Patty Duke. She believed me and cut my hair to my neck. I just knew that this would bring me peace. This would let me finally fit in and be like other black girls. It worked, at least I thought, for a brief period. Liz's sister informed their mother what had happened at the park and her mother reported to all of the mothers. The girls were forced by their mothers to apologize. I do not know how much trouble they got into. I forgave them and we played together, but it was not like before, especially for my dark skinned friend, who had for the most part ignored me.

By the time I was ten years old, my father was out of the 'family picture', my older siblings were busy working and preparing for college while my younger brother was bored with school and getting in trouble. Randall was very bright academically and could learn quickly. But, like me, he had too many distractions at home, and coped the only way he knew how. Later, in his teens Randall would drop out of high school and become heavily involved in drugs and gambling. Drugs and gambling would almost cost him his life when he was left for dead in three different incidents. He was saved by the ray of hope in Jesus, and given a new life and a second chance. I am proud of my brother, Randall who has long been set free of alcohol and has never turned back. His time now is focusing on ministry. Randall and I lived a different kind of life from our older siblings. We both lived within our family when our parents were at their worst. Our older brother and sister did not experience the dark things we did.

I was lost without the consistent support of a mother. Most of the time, she was too tired, too intoxicated, or too stressed. The day I was diagnosed with the glaucoma trait, she had had a few drinks and went into an emotional breakdown that I would eventually become blind. Honestly, I was more upset with the idea that I was near-sighted and would have to wear eyeglasses. The greatest fear for me was attracting attention with these cat-eye shaped frames. There was no way I would voluntarily make myself vulnerable. I decided to not wear my glasses and wearing them only at home. I decided that not seeing was far better than being humiliated, and once again rejected.

The 70's brought me a sense of belonging with the black power movement. We were no longer calling ourselves colored. Dashikis, Afros, Afro puffs and cornbraids were common expressions of being natural, and identifying with our heritage roots from Africa. My hair had almost grown fully back, forcing me to use 70 small sponge curlers to get a Fro. Blackness was something beautiful and something to respect.

My mother had experienced such intra-racial negativity within her own home as a child and teenager, that she was determined to make sure that her children would love and respect any shade of black. One year my mother had taken me and my brother to her office Christmas party. It was a very big function. I remember the huge Christmas tree, and the never-ending tables of food. My mother was one of four black employees in the entire laboratory institute. As we were leaving for the evening, one of her Caucasian co-workers brushed my hair with her hands and said to my mother that I had such soft hair and was a very pretty child. My mother responded with a half-smile and was quiet until we got home. I sensed that she was disturbed. She declared to us both, "Looks and hair don't ever make a person better than another one. It doesn't matter if one is light, dark, or brown; and there is no such thing as good hair. God made all hair; and all hair is good." Years later she revealed to me that she was upset that Christmas night because it was suggested that dark skinned blacks with curly or nappy hair aren't very pretty. Then she told me how her father showed biased in their family to the lighter skinned siblings. She and her middle sister were darker and treated unfairly. My mother would have to use a hot comb on her hair when it was fashionable to have a smooth look. I valued my mother's words never forgetting them. It is a bit ironic that I never really thought myself pretty or having good hair, yet most of my negative intra-racial experiences centered on just that.

I was now in the fifth grade. I would eventually end up having attended two elementary schools, one middle school, and two high schools. In spite of everything, fifth grade was my best school year. I truly respected and admired my teacher. He was my greatest teacher. Mr. Sodderd was a young white male from South Boston who was passionate about teaching and shaping the minds of his students, no matter the color. Four years from this time, South Boston would become nationally infamous for its racist anti-desegregation position. Our class was predominantly comprised of blacks, sprinkled with whites, Asians and Latinos. I believe it was Mr. Sodderd's mission to make us think beyond what we thought we could do. Our brains were the muscles he wanted us to flex daily. One time he gave us an assignment with the word antidis-establishmentarianism. He made sure we knew what it meant. It was a political position that originated in 19th-century Britain that opposed the *disestablishment* of the Church of England which would remove its' status as *the state church* of *England*. Mr. Sodderd challenged us to produce the most words out of this one word in three days.

This was music to my ears! I did not wait a second to start seeing words and writing them down. He gave us three days to turn in our words. It was another good distraction to tune out my home life. I spent almost every minute at home discovering words. We were allowed to use the dictionary. The day after the assignment had been turned in, a classmate told me to get to the homeroom before recess was over. I thought what did I do, I never got in trouble. My mother taught us to respect all authority. She warned us that if we disrespected any teacher then we would get punished again at home with a spanking or as we called it, a whooping to our behinds. I made sure I was never to be called to a teacher's room or principal's office. When I got to my homeroom Mr. Sodderd told me to have a seat. He smiled and said you won with 230 words! He then handed me a prize, a brand new cassette recorder with a new cassette! I cherished this recorder and had it for many years.

Mr. Sodderd was also sensitive to our need to have pride in ourselves as individuals and as a member of the Black race. He allowed us to express ourselves without censoring our blackness. During lunch one day, we were feeling very black and very proud. Someone started to sing the unofficial black anthem. Dark skinned, light skinned, brown skinned, even some of the white students joined in, singing and parading around the room, "Ungowa, Ungowa, this means Black Power, Black Power, I said it, I meant it, I really represent it. It takes a cool cool sister from a cool cool town…it takes a cool cool brother from a cool cool town, you don't like my act you don't shake me tree, so listen mister mister don't mess with me". Mr. Sodderd looked up from his newspaper, took a bite from his apple, smiled and just let us be black...and be proud.

It was a few months before school ended and it would have been a full school year without a major incident. Then out of the blue, a classmate told me to be careful after school because a girl named Kayla in the sixth grade wanted to 'kick my behind' because I looked at her. Back in the day, you could be called into a fight for merely looking at someone. I should have told Mr. Sodderd. He would have protected me. I guess keeping drama and danger to myself became a hard habit to break. I was not a fighter and definitely did not want to get beaten up. Yet, I had to leave the classroom and meet my brother at the entrance. When the dreaded school bell rang at 2:30, I was terrified. A crowd of kids had gathered in front of the school, ready to witness a fight. There standing tall and much bigger than me, was a dark skinned girl named Kayla. She told me to hurry up and knock the stick off her shoulder. It was an urban ritual that meant the fight would now commence. Of course, I was not going to knock anything off anyone's shoulder. I did not want the fight to ever begin. Kayla got right in my face, "What are you looking at? You think you're so cute; you and your rat straight hair". Before I could say a word, she punched me in the forehead. My head went back. Kayla thought that was good enough and walked away with her friends. The pain in my head was throbbing and would not stop. My three homeroom friends (two dark skinned and one brown skinned) had been too afraid to stop the fight, but they stayed with me until my brother's third grade class came out. He saw my head and exclaimed the obvious, that I had a big lump on my head. The obvious lump meant that I would have to tell my mother, giving her something else to worry about.

As my brother and I got two seats on the subway, I kept trying to figure out what got people so angry with me. I cut my hair, but that made no difference. I tried being in the sun when it was hot so I could get tanned, get darker, and that did not matter. When my mother got home from work she asked me what happened. Lying was not an option. My mother had instilled three important values into my being: never steal, never cheat, and never lie. So, it would be the truth that a girl said I looked at her; that she punched me, and that she said that I had rat hair and that I thought I was cute. My mother held me and let me cry in her arms. I felt so protected in her arms; the emotional hurt and physical pain of that afternoon started to dissipate. She assured me that she loved me so very much, and said that she was sorry, and it's a shame that we blacks have so much anger and take it out on each other. She tucked me in bed, told me to say my bedtime prayer, and then kissed me goodnight.

Kayla never touched me again. She never even said a word to me…and that was quite okay with me. I tend to think that my mother told Mr. Sodderd. If she did, then I know he took action. All was good again and I finished the fifth grade with no fear of being jumped after school and my hard work paid off with getting on the honor roll! Unfortunately, it would be my last year at this school. In order for us to be closer to home, my mother enrolled us in a Catholic school in Mission Hill. What bad timing; just when I had a few school friends and was beginning to find myself, I would now have to start over again and be lost again.

It was my brother Randall who introduced me to the new neighborhood, to basketball and to church. He never seemed timid about meeting new people and just went with the flow. He played basketball and encouraged me to go with him. I saw girls my age 12 and older playing just as well, and even better than some of the guys. I was intrigued and wanted to learn. Basketball had become my new past time. It was a place where instead of girls being petty, girls were sticking together improving their game so they could be competitive enough to be picked up, to be selected on a team. Being picked up was one of the greatest compliments in street basketball. One of the girls I played with was dark skinned and had the most radiant smile that lit up every space she entered. Her brother had previously invited Randall to their church and she later extended the invitation to me. My brother and I went with her mother and siblings to church for almost three years. Cindy had befriended me and invited me to her home. I trusted her and saw that she was genuine. I think we connected because we had the same driven mentality. We both went to the basketball court every day to better our game and perfecting our lay ups and hook shots. We both knew somehow, someway that we would go to college. Her mother had become another mom to us and her family had become our family. We became cousins.

Being in Cindy's home was a respite away from my mother' drinking and self-pity. Our friendship has been life-long to this day. It was refreshing to not speculate a friendship's based on the shade of our blackness. My light complexion and long hair was no longer a topic for me—at least not until college.

The middle school years was the period in my life when I began to find myself through the discovery of a first genuine friendship, a first experience with God, and a first love—basketball. I would need these firsts to bring me through the waves of crisis that would crash through my vulnerable world.

CHAPTER FIVE

ELEPHANTS IN THE ROOM

We are hard pressed on every side, but not crushed;
perplexed, but not in despair; persecuted, but not abandoned;
struck down, but not destroyed

—2 Corinthians 4:8-9

Elephants are very big and that is an under statement. Male elephants can weigh up to 12,000-14,000 pounds with an average height of thirteen feet. Elephants in their enormity do not always know when they have crushed or struck down something in their path. The metaphorical idiom "elephant in the room" represents an obvious fact, problem, or risk that is ignored and unaddressed. Essentially, this elephant is a problem that no one wants to admit or discuss. Alcoholism was one of the elephants in the room of my mother's home. Depression and anger were the other elephants. As big as these elephants were and the damage they did, my mother never admitted she had a problem. Since she refused to acknowledge her condition and its consequences, that meant that none of us could bring it to her attention. She would respond that she really doesn't drink much and that it relaxes her. Both of these were lies. She drank a lot and when she drank she was far from relaxed. Her drinking escalated her current emotion. She drank everyday. I stopped counting the glasses and began counting the empty bottles. Randall stopped emptying her alcohol in the toilet when he realized that she would borrow money to replace it. It was always a vain attempt. My mother drank when she was sad, happy, upset, depressed. The worst was seeing her over the years when she was drinking with her male companions; they would talk loud, talk slurred and talk foolishly.

It was never a good option talking to my mother about her drinking. The repercussion of her getting more upset was usually followed by more drinking.

The cycle of addiction is vicious. Once a person begins to think beyond their denial, it becomes frightening to encounter the truth. There is the truth about the horrible behavior and habits that have resulted from abusive drinking. My mother would have had to deal with the truth of her perceptions that her marriage was a failure, that her husband was a failure and that she was a failure. There were a few occasions when I would come home and find my mother crying on the sofa with her drink on the coffee table. She would speak about her failures to me. I was just a kid and felt awkward in those moments trying to console her the best way I knew, telling her that she had so much going for herself and that she had so much to give.

My mother drank to escape from her unresolved issues of her past and unresolved relationships of the present. These open wounds caused her to act out with a self-destructive behavior. Once an addicted person admits their problem, they hone in on the shame and embarrassment. This guilt develops into despair...

which leads back to the destructive behavior. Thus the cycle of addiction repeats. I wish my mother had known the difference between the admission of her drinking problem and the confession of her sin. She would have known that once she confesses her bad behavior, her self-destructive activity, her selfishness, her anger and her overall weakness, God would forgive it all, wiping her slate squeaky clean. Because once forgiven, it is done.

> *"If we confess our sins, he is faithful and just and will forgive us our sins and purify us from all unrighteousness."*
>
> —1 JOHN 1:9

She would have known that the Lord Jesus loved her right where she was and that it did not matter what others thought. She would have known that it is good to love yourself, and to forgive yourself.

I learned in seminary that addiction comprises three natures: the neurological nature, the psychological nature, and the Spiritual nature. The *neurological nature* involves the brain and body in which the neuroreceptors are sensitive to internal and external stimuli. We possess internal body-produced hormone chemicals. Nicotine, caffeine and other drugs are external chemical agents that travel through the bloodstream. *The psychological nature* involves our capacity to choose and to determine how to behave. The *Spiritual Nature* is the place where we lose our freedom through the bondage of something. Most theologians concur that addiction of any kind, is the displacement of Spiritual longing. In other words, when a person becomes addicted she obsesses over that thing or activity. She is desperately trying to satisfy her hunger for God with something else. *The addiction is the idol that replaces God.* Addiction imprisoned my mother to the behavior of her drinking compulsion and to her preoccupation with sadness and regret. When people become wounded they act out, and many wounded persons participate in destructive over-consumptive behaviors that could involve food, chocolate, social media, pornography, sex, power, work, drugs, gambling or alcohol. My mother did not have the tools of knowledge nor the faith, to confess her abusive drinking. Alcohol was her choice of drug and denial was her place of comfort.

Denial is perplexing. Our entire family knew the problem existed, yet everyone had to act like there was no problem. There is an unwritten rule, an unofficial family code of ethics that dictates that 'our secrets stay our secrets, and all we have to do is ignore the issue and it will take care of itself.' I felt like my family situation 'was what it was' and there was nothing I could do to change the situation. I was hard-pressed, emotionally struck down, but never destroyed.

My mother's alcoholism and Tony's institutionalism were family secrets that I was determined to keep secret. The shame and embarrassment were too much for me to handle and I would do anything to avoid any more humiliation. I would no longer invite friends to my home. I would never tell anyone about my mother's drinking. The best solution for me was to continue to flee from the elephant…to continue to be away from my home as much as possible trying to find love, peace and security in relationships. It was always easier said than done, because I made it difficult for myself. There were very few things that I had control over during my teen years, so I decided to control as much as I could in my life by protecting myself from any vulnerability. The only way I knew how, was to continue to keep the people I knew away from my home, and to keep my thoughts and softer side hidden. Control was my secret weapon…or so I thought.

A robot is a mechanical device that sometimes resembles a human, yet does not possess feelings, but is capable of performing a variety of complex human tasks on command. By the time I was fifteen, I had developed robotic attributes. I seldom expressed sadness and fear. When I did cry, it was usually behind closed doors. Such emotions and feelings were too costly. If I were to spend time thinking about the elephants in the room, sadness and depression could have become my focus at the expense of my scholastic goals. A successful college education was too precious to me; it would provide me choices. Sadness had great potential to slow me down or to destroy me like my mother. She wore sadness daily and it had become her favorite outfit. I had no desire to live and wear depression, nor did I want to seek refuge in drugs or alcohol. The devil makes such destructive devices easy to find and to obtain. That was not in my playbook for success. I was on a mission. That mission was for me to get out…get out of my home, get out of my neighborhood and eventually get out of Massachusetts. I thought that movement away from home would solve my life problems.

When I took on this semi-numb existence of keeping sadness at bay and feelings tucked away, I unknowingly sacrificed joy, humor and laughter. I was becoming far too serious about almost everything. Jokes were not just jokes, but commentaries that I had to first process and then rethink. Sarcastic people were close to repulsive to me because sarcasm was a fool's lack of courage to speak the direct truth. When I was thirteen we had capping sessions on our neighborhood basketball court where one person hurls funny insults on another person, then vice versa. Unlike bullying, capping involved willing participants who volunteered to 'cap' or be 'capped on'. If you didn't want to cap then you had to be quiet and stay in the back. We all wanted to be a part of it because after we were the butt of the joke, we could get someone else. Sometimes things were said making the kids in the crowd laugh hysterically. I had fun capping because even though it was tough, it was honest, but not cruel. As much as this was out of my comfort zone, I thought that this would prove that I could take it, I could 'hang' and be part of the group. It worked for a little while.

As I became more involved in high school with my studies and sports, I outgrew the need to be part of a group. I was at the age where most of the girls I knew had boyfriends. I, however, never got the attention of boys my age. I probably never gave them a chance, maybe because of my introverted nature, intense exterior and insecurity. I was nervous around boys that I liked, not confident enough to look at them in the face. So how at the age of 15, did I end up with a 21 year-old as my boyfriend for almost two years? Same old, but sad story…older guys are attracted to young girls because they can take advantage and manipulate them. Younger girls appeal to older types because they seek a father-figure hoping to obtain the love they did not get as a little girl. Bobby was that figure, but also a bad boy type. I did not know just how bad until several months into the relationship. He was handsome and knew how to work his looks and charm on everyone, even my mother. I never knew why she allowed me to have a relationship with Bobby; maybe because I always acted mature for my age and I was responsible. Maybe she just didn't care; maybe she wanted me happy. Whatever her reason, it was all part of the distorted dysfunction in my life.

My cousin Cindy and I would walk past the billiards game room every day after summer day camp in our work clothes–shorts, sneakers and ugly t-shirts. We were camp counselors. Like clockwork, Bobby would invite us to play pool. The first few asks we said no, because he looked older, and because we had no clue how to shoot pool. Temptation eventually got its way. We soon hung out every day learning to master our pool shots and delving deeper into a world of seedy characters. One day Bobby asked if I would like to be his lady. Naïve, I gladly accepted, not realizing that it would compromise my virginity, and jeopardize my independence. Bobby had repeatedly asked me to give in sexually. I did not mind kissing, but I was not ready for that experience. He made a comment once that he never had a virgin. He said it as if it was a great conquest. I gave in reluctantly. The experience is one I regretted then, and still regret. I wished I had preserved my virginal integrity for the man that God would have me to marry.

It should have been a red flag for me, but I was too lost in 'love' or what I thought was love. There were many other red flags, but when you're young and blind, you cannot see the signs. Loser was written all over him: he lived with his mother; he smoked marijuana and Hashish; he was a pool hustler, and he had a gun. He tried to entice me a few times to indulge in drugs. It was God's grace and my self-control that prevented me from going down that path with Bobby. When he tried to persuade me from going to college, my eyes were wide open. I now *saw* the dark side of him. I was nothing more to him than just something else to say he got. I asked him once if he had other women, he said no. It was in that moment that I grew up quickly. Nights that I was home studying he was 'playing the field' with women his age. I actually went down one night to catch him in one of his many lies. I did not say anything to him. I kept it to myself for several weeks until my school exams were over, and then I approached him with my final 'speech' lasting about five minutes. I told him that no one or nothing would ever stop me from going to college, and he was welcome to have as many women as he desired because we were through, and I never ever wanted to see him again. I meant every word I said that day. Two years later, he knocked on my mother's door asking for me. He put on his usual charm and she let him in. When I saw him I told him to never come to my house again, or I would call the police. I despised him. I despised what I *allowed* him to take from me. I *allowed* him to take my virginity, my dignity, my self-respect, and almost my future. *Lesson learned, but not retained.*

When I had left Commonwealth High School during my brother Tony's mental instability, I left at the height and heat of Boston's infamous desegregation ruling. It was not a good time to enroll in any of Boston's public high schools. Inner-city kids were violently acting out because the racist white parents of Dorchester were violent against the black students who were now forced enrollees in 'their' schools. Predominantly black schools in Boston were putting white students' heads in toilets; beating them and knifing some. I refused to be around this tension so I stayed out of school for a month. I had no real option until my sister Denise and her husband offered me to live with them in the suburbs to attend high school. It was a great option, in more ways than I could have imagined. I would be away from home during the week until the weekends. I could play high school basketball again. The down side was that I was now starting over with meeting new 'friends'; I had no money for my incidentals and I had no transportation to get back and forth to Boston. The answer for me was to find a job and get a cheap car. I also tried out for the varsity team. The coach selected me for guard position and then rescinded when I told her that I would miss practice one day a week because I had to work at a bakery after school. I had been honest and believed that I had been penalized because I did not have the luxury not to work. My brother-in-law owned a gas station mechanic shop and sold me a station wagon for five hundred dollars, allowing me to pay over time.

A friend from church asked me if I needed more work and I said yes…yes to working as a waitress 'paid under the table', paid cash off the grid. The reason for this was because I was sixteen years old working illegally in a nightclub. Other than tasting a few of the drinks before the club opened, I had no desire to drink. I was there to work, not socialize. If we chose to make more tips then we would have had to dress like the other waitresses. My friend assured me that if I followed her lead, all would be well with no compromise. The two of us dressed conservatively always in pants and buttoned shirts almost to our necks. I was not about to become something else just for a tip. I only needed enough money to pay for my weekly gas and small expenses.

After almost five months of working every Friday and Saturday night, it came to an end on New Year's Eve. Up to this point, I had never been involved in a club incident. I had been instructed that if anyone was threatening me that I was to let Big Marv know. He was the club's bouncer, big and mean; but he was a teddy bear to us, always kind and polite. On this night, a customer lied and said I had owed him more change. He got ugly and in my face. I signaled to Big Marv and a big scene soon followed because the customer refused to back down. Big Marv threw him out. The guy looked at me and said, "Watch yourself." I decided then that this was my last night; little did I know that this was one of the most dangerous clubs in Boston. Shootings occurred regularly. Drugs were a part of the scene and so on… It just so happened that these things never happened the weekends I was working. I took for granted God's divine protection.

Bobby had been out of my life for almost a year. I was almost seventeen and soon graduating from high school. I had no interest in boys my age. The bad part is that a few nice guys really liked me. I did not know what to do with them, nor did I want to explain or even discuss my family or my mother. As much as I missed her, I would avoid her and say very little when I came home to Boston on the weekends. Near the end of the school year, I was coming home maybe once a month. I was focusing on school and finding a real love, someone that really cared for me. Older guys had become my poison. The pattern was set. I truly believed the lie that an older man could fill all the voids in my life. Between March and August I dated four guys between the ages nineteen and 24. Again, I allowed them to take from me without them ever wanting to give me what I needed. Lesson learned and this time the lesson was retained.

By the end of the summer I was pretty much done with dating and put my energy into preparing for college. Thanks to the Carter administration, government college loans and grants were readily available for poverty-level students like me. I applied to only two colleges. It was not that I was so sure of myself; it was ignorance. My mother did not know that I should apply to at least five colleges. My high school guidance counselor was a racist and provided me with minimal college preparation; however, she was a "nice racist" who would probably say that she was not a racist, and that Afro-Americans were good people. I had come from one of the best private high schools with good grades but the first time we met she strongly suggested that I take business classes and typing classes. I defended my grades and college goals, telling her that I wanted to take at least two honor classes my junior year. I also told her that I anticipated becoming a physical therapist. She said that I would not be a good prospect since I would not be able to handle the math and science coursework in college. She never encouraged me to take additional math or science classes to prepare for my last year and a half, or to get tutoring, or to take additional summer classes. She only reminded me that I would have to take evening classes to make up the month I lost when I was in-between schools during Boston's desegregation. She was supposed to be my guidance counselor, yet I received no guidance. I was not privy to the tricks of the trade for college preparation. I had no idea that I could take the Scholastic Aptitude Tests more than once to improve my score. My SAT score was low particularly in the areas of math and science. No surprise. My school grade point average was good (not spectacular). I am grateful to Mr. Merrill who came through on his promise to give me an outstanding recommendation. My miracle came through when I received my letter of admission to Boston University! This poor girl from Roxbury, Back Bay and Mission Hill was embarking on doing something great with her life…a life that the Lord protected from all harm and danger. When Lot was told to flee to the mountains or he will be swept away, he said to the angels of the Lord, "…Your servant has found favor in your eyes, and you have shown great kindness to me in sparing my life!" I, like Lot, was unworthy, yet my Lord had mercy on me and had a purpose for my life. The elephants had hard pressed me but had not destroyed me.

Boston University was only about three miles from my home in Mission Park, yet it was a whole new world. I was confident that my world was going to change for the better. I knew what it would take to succeed at this institution—hard work. College was my key out of the hood. A lot of kids I knew had ended up pregnant, into drugs, or dropping out of school. I hardly deviated from my school work. I was intensely focused and did not pay attention to the usual freshman distractions like boys and parties. So when my roommate invited me to the Sleeper Hall 'break jam', I hesitated. These 'break jams' were impromptu party moments by one of the student DJ's known as CC or the Chocolate Cowboy. Fifteen or twenty minutes tops were the gist of these breaks. As fun as they were, I would always rush back to the library after only ten minutes. Every time when I left, this one guy would throw me the line, "You're fine and you're all mine." I totally ignored him. I was not thinking about boys. I really did not care and had no use for them. It was about the third time when he followed me down the hall and said it again. I guess he thought I should have been impressed because I was a freshman and he was a sophomore. That was not it at all. Something just resonated with me because of his humor and his sincerity. I turned to him and told him he was silly. He said his name was Jeffrey and walked me to my dorm. The next time we spoke was about a month later. He came by my room on Halloween and we talked while sitting at the end of my bed. We actually talked until two a.m. never once sharing a physical intimate exchange. The conversation was far from trivial. We shared the challenges and dysfunctions in our young lives and spoke about why we were determined to succeed in college. While excelling in his high school honor classes, Jeffrey was an all-star athlete in track, football and basketball. He was offered several football scholarships, which led him to B.U. We began dating and two months later I met his family and he met mine. That summer Jeffrey proposed to me and gave me a pre-engagement ring. We agreed that nothing would get in the way of our degrees and that our wedding would be after we both graduated. We kept our promise.

Jeffrey was the best thing that had ever happened to me and for the first time, I experienced a real love, a true love, a meaningful love. But the road to the altar did not come without life's drama. The second year into our relationship, I became pregnant. I took precautions using an IUD, however I was not aware of its high risk for pregnancy. God was not yet invited into my life as my Lord. I knew the bible was His book, yet I had no desire to read it. I did not know how those words on those pages could be alive, could relate just to me, could heal my brokenness…could protect me.

> *"For this is the will of God, your sanctification: that you abstain from sexual immorality; that each one of you know how to control his own body in holiness and honor,"*
>
> —1 Thessalonians 4:3-4, ESV

I did not appreciate God's word on abstinence and that it was out of his love and his protection for us that he instructs both male and female to wait. What most men and women do not recognize is that sexual intimacy creates a mental connection that our brain never forgets. Whether men and women want to accept this or not, it is a fact that this mental connection establishes an emotional bond. This is why so many women are hurt when a one-night-stand goes sour and in the morning when her 'perfect date' says he has to go and will call her later, but never does. It is the same for men when a woman decides to avoid his calls after a first sexual encounter. The male usually battles his ego by licking the wounds of his pride and seemingly moves on. But like a woman, he moves on with the same hurt and tucks it away. If we could only see that God understands our struggles, he made our body, he created our sexual desires, yet he provided us with the power to control them…the power of the Holy Spirit. He gave us this power through the gift of his sacrificed Son, Jesus the Christ, and when we operate in this power, it is life-changing and life-giving.

> *"Now to him who is able to do immeasurably more than all we can ask or imagine according to his power that is at work within us,"*

—EPHESIANS 3:20

My fiancé Jeffrey and I were in love, but love is not the ok button for sexual intimacy. Any act of God's disobedience brings consequence. I regret that I did not read God's Holy word. I regret that I did not heed the sacred words of 1 Thessalonians. I regret that I did not abstain from sexual immorality even with the man that I would be married to for 33 years. If I had obeyed God's word I would not have had to deal with the trauma of an abortion in my second year at B.U. In my desperate and selfish state, I made a horrific decision…to take the life of an innocent baby. Although the world said abortion is no big deal and that it's only a fetus, I felt something wrong as soon as I rose from the table. I immediately felt nauseous, not from the procedure, but from the realization of what I had just done. I no longer believed that abortion was merely the termination of a fetus. I knew that I had just killed a baby that was alive inside my womb. I kept this dark secret to myself, telling no one except Jeffrey. It was a sad day for both of us. The decision to have an abortion would haunt me for many years.

In the midst of the downs, college life had many ups for me. I had been invited to two of the Black Sorority interviews for line pledging. I declined because I was a MePhiMe. I was too independent and rebellious to last a hot minute pledging, especially with its potential hazing. I was adamant about the idea of servanthood or anything resembled any remnant of slavery. Years later this became another regret of mine. I was in my thirties when I finally appreciated the contributions that our African American Sororities and Fraternities made to its communities with the vehicles of networks, mentorships, civic contributions and financial support. It is indeed an honor to have these institutions a part of our heritage framework. One of my roommates went Greek. Both roommates were great friends and great study partners—one was the pretty color of expresso and the other a shade of mocha. I was so grateful that my color and hair was not a topic of discussion, at least not in most circles at college. Boston University did not accept as many African Americans compared to the Caucasian and foreign student population. The various cultures naturally segregated themselves, including us Black students. Common language, common mores, common history and common struggles were the impetus. It was how we blacks could positively cope with racism and its bigotry. I became active in student organizations like the Black Student Union called Umoja which meant unity, and Black Expressions which was the School of Public Communications black communicators' organization. I became the advertising manager and co-editor of *Blackfolk*, which was our campus and community newspaper. Most of us were well-connected to B.U.'s Martin Luther King Jr. Center, under the direction of the minority student dean, Reverend Dr. Conley Hughes who created an environment of an emotional safe haven on campus for black students. It was a place to come for our concerns, our passions, our celebrations, and a place to just come and do nothing but be black.

In 1978, racism was very much alive. Jeffrey on his way from the library, about to enter his campus apartment, was stopped by the Boston police. They drove up on the sidewalk. Two white officers told him to put his hands down on the police car and had him spread eagle. His books, papers and keys fell to the ground. Jeffrey knew to be compliant. He told them that he was a B.U. student and that he had his student I.D. Once they saw his I.D. they said he fit the description of a rapist in the area. That was all the police said. They let him go without an apology and left him to collect his fallen items. At one of our student "get-togethers," a friend told us how every night her white roommate would stare at her when she got ready for bed. She finally asked her what she was looking at. The white girl asked her what happened to her tail. Her daddy said that all blacks have tails and some have cut them off. My friend was in shock and told her roommate that she and her daddy were crazy! We later found out that the white student was from the south. Her only exposure to black people was through television, and prior to college, she had never been in the presence of a black person. Our common struggle and racist experiences on campus kept the intra-racial bite at bay. With the exception of questions about my heritage: "Am I half-black? Do I know how to cook grits or collard greens? Do I know how to dance?" I for the most part experienced a brother-sister bond with the blacks on campus, and it was a satisfying feeling. After a few years of marriage, Jeffrey informed me that there were several guys in college who wanted to ask me for a date, but thought I was a stuck up light-skinned, uppity black. They mostly misread my intense focus on schoolwork and lack of confidence, as such. Even in college I did not know how to look directly at folks especially males. I would walk by fast or look down or just ignore. It is amazing that Jeffrey saw something beyond that, and decided to risk and ask. I'm grateful he took that chance.

I did not have much of a social life in college. Most of my time was spent in the library. That is where Jeffrey knew to find me the day he told me to come quickly and that we were taking a cab to my mother's home. I knew something was wrong. He told me that my sister found my mother dead. I cannot imagine what it would have been like without Jeffrey there with me. He was my rock. When I arrived at her home, she was lying on the living room couch. The coffee table had a few of her home remedies displayed showing her attempt to cure what she thought was the flu. My mother's body looked as if she had been burned. There was no coroner to be found. It was Saturday and the excuse was that the city could not get one to our house because it was the weekend. It would be six hours later before the coroner's arrival. For six hours we agonized over her appearance and agonized imagining what had happened to her. Monday the coroner's report stated that her death was pneumonia due to alcohol abuse. Alcoholics are predisposed to lung infections like pneumonia. I had guilt because I did not visit her as much as I should have. I had believed that I could have prevented her death by convincing her to go the hospital. I also thought that she had betrayed me by cutting her life short at fifty four with her addiction. She was now gone forever. She would not watch me graduate the next year or walk down the aisle on my wedding day. The funeral was oblivious to me. I don't remember much. I took incompletes for all of my coursework and spent the next three months away from school at my sisters' house. I felt broken beyond repair. I had a deep infinite hole that kept spiraling down into my soul, never to be filled. I woke up for months dreaming of my mother as if she were still alive. I anticipated seeing her at home. A few times I thought I saw her walking across the street. I was in the shock phase of her death. It was surreal. I needed a respite from my reality. At one point I was going to withdraw from school because I was emotionally tired and ready to quit. Instead, I decided to press on for my mother's sake, as she had taught me that hard work meant something, and that I could not ever quit. When I returned to school, I was still grieving. It was extremely difficult and almost impossible to finish my incomplete assignments while working on the current ones, yet I did it! I did not quit and the following year I graduated right on schedule with a Bachelor of Science degree in Broadcasting and Film. My dream was to help the world by writing and producing social documentaries. The dream never became a reality.

CHAPTER SIX

A PILLAR OF SALT

You are the salt of the earth. But if the salt loses its saltiness, how can it be made salty again? It is no longer good for anything, except to be thrown out and trampled underfoot

—Matthew 5:13

A great cook was my mother; nothing gourmet, just good ole fashioned great, tasty and exceptionally flavorful food. Everything that makes me a great cook is because I watched my mother, and she had learned from her mother-in-law. It does not matter if you live in the north, the south, the east or the west, macaroni and cheese and collard greens are staple foods in the African American culture. It is the center piece dish of every holiday and a celebrated tradition, and boy oh boy, could my mother make your mouth water for more and more, even if your belly felt like it was about to pop! Four different cheeses, cream of mushroom, butter, and a bit of salt melted so perfectly that the creamy cheese would drizzle on your palate. Her collard greens that had simmered for hours seasoned with ham hocks, vinegar, pepper and salt could never get better. Salt is a natural enhancer releasing its good flavor into the food. Salt is also a useful preservative. It has the dual ability to let go or to keep.

The pillar of salt in Genesis illustrates how Lot's wife was locked in forever. Her saltiness and usefulness was forever gone. By the time I was in college, my mother's cooking fell into the experimental category. I would never know if her meal would be the great "mouth-watering flavorful to-die-for dish" or if it would be something she would "try different". If it fell into the latter one, then it was usually a disaster and it was usually when she had been drinking. She hit a home run with her true-blue mac and cheese and collards the day I invited Jeffrey to meet her. She indulged with minimal alcohol that day. I was relieved of being embarrassed, and I was proud of her self-control. She also hit a home run with Jeffrey. They connected like mother and son in an instant. It was these kind of days that had made me smile, that had me hope for my mother. A hope short-lived. She went back to her usual ways, usual drinking and usual uselessness. Her flavor was gone. She let herself become a pillar of salt...a pillar of bitterness, anger and resentment. Little did I know that I was heading in the same direction, slowly turning into a pillar of salt.

Jeffrey graduated the year my mother died. It was bittersweet attending his graduation because she was not there and because she adored and loved him. Without my knowledge, he had showed her the pre-engagement ring telling her of his marriage intentions. She was elated. My mother would have been at his graduation and would have wanted the entire family over for one of her savory meals. Salt was beginning to lose its flavor in me as well. I think I was slowly dying, at least emotionally. After Jeffrey's graduation, he moved to Austin, Texas to find a job in communications. He actually worked two jobs to help pay for the wedding and honeymoon. I moved off campus and lived with my roommate. It was a major challenge for me to finish that year. I was lonely and at times very depressed. Like most of my emotions, I was an expert at hiding my depression. Happiness would come when I was preparing for the wedding. My sister Denise, took on the role of my mother in assisting me in all of the preparations including the wedding shower. She had sewn my wedding dress (more beautiful than I had imagined) replicating my mother's wedding gown which was absolutely stunning! The wedding day finally arrived in August; another bittersweet occasion. The one person I longed to be at my side was again absent. My father arrived late and a bit intoxicated. When Jeffrey and I flew off to our honeymoon, I was beyond happy, thinking that my world was now wonderful and brand new! I would be moving to Texas; I could put my past behind me!

Most of my young adult years were void of dialogue or thought regarding God, religion or church. The times that I did attend church, were good while they lasted and then I would forget about them. Newly wed, Jeffrey and I rarely mentioned God. Our conversations centered on securing work and making a life for ourselves in Austin. God knows the paths that we eventually take. I believe God has an unconditional and undying love while he patiently waits for us to come full-circle, and love him back. In the fourth month of our marriage I woke up one Sunday morning with an overwhelming desire to go to church. Every Sunday after, I woke up with the same urgent desire. I finally told Jeffrey that I did not know why, but I needed to visit a church. Amazingly, he said yes and asked his best friend where we should visit. We visited one church and after two months of visiting David Chapel Missionary Baptist Church, we became members. On that Sunday, the Pastor said the "church of the doors are now open." I had absolutely no idea what that meant. But my heart pressured me to go to the altar. Jeffrey came right behind me and said that someone had nudged him. After the excitement of accepting Jesus as our Lord and Savior, Jeffrey discovered that there was not anyone sitting behind him. No one had nudged him. We acknowledged that it was the Holy Spirit that nudged us, that moved us, that convicted us.

It was God's plan that we join his kingdom and this church family at that very instant!

> *"But God demonstrates his own love for us in this: While we were still sinners, Christ died for us."*
>
> —ROMANS 5:8

God our creator has birthed a spiritual connection in all of us, his creatures.

> *"For you created my inmost being; you knit me together in my mother's womb."*
>
> —PSALM 139:13

It is our willingness to acknowledge him, to acknowledge his love and his Lordship over our lives. Out of love and obedience for our Savior, we were then baptized.

> *"Therefore go and make disciples of all nations, baptizing them in the name of the Father, and of the Son and of the Holy Spirit, and teaching them to obey everything I have commanded you."*
>
> —MATTHEW 28:19-20

David Chapel Missionary Baptist Church became our home, our family and a place where we discovered the way, the truth and the life in Jesus, the risen Christ.

It was the sermons, the bible classes and fellowship in which God grew me. At about the end of that first year of our marriage, God spoke to me in his Word one day, while I was at home thinking about the abortion. Tears of guilt and sadness rolled down my cheeks non-stop when I thought about that precious baby God had created in me. That fetus even at six weeks was a baby, with the nose, mouth and ears taking shape. The eyes and nostrils had started to form, as had the arms and legs. Its' precious heart beat about 100 to 160 times per minute, and its blood had begun to course through its tiny one inch body. I had nowhere else to turn except to God's word.

> *"For I will forgive their wickedness and will remember their sins no more."*
>
> —HEBREWS 8:12

I got on my knees and cried out to God, "Please forgive me for taking a life that belonged to you. Lord, forgive me for my evil deed, in Jesus name, Amen." After the prayer, my tears now flowed because of the inner-joy and peace I had received knowing that I was forgiven, and that my God has no record of it! I believed it then, and I continued to walk in that assurance, because my God does not lie, my God does not break a promise, my God does not hold me hostage to my past! I had been released of that burden of guilt by just getting on my knees and asking for forgiveness! It was that simple. To this day, I have never experienced guilt or shame for the abortion. My Lord and Savior, judge and redeemer had liberated me. This was one great moment where I never looked back!

After two years of marriage, I wanted a baby. I had a position as Municipal Access Producer for the City of Austin. It was a far cry from social documentaries, but I was writing speeches for the Mayor, editing, directing and producing the three camera live tapings of the various council and planning commission meetings. Most importantly, I was a city employee with health benefits. Jeffrey had not yet secured work in his field with benefits. So I was more than ready to have six children like my maternal grandparents. Jeffrey wanted to wait until his job was more secure. I was relentless. I could not wait to hold a baby of my own in my arms. Jeffrey succumbed and we had our first born, Corey. Jeffrey was a great daddy-to-be, attending every Lamaze class. He was right by my side the entire thirteen long hours of labor. He then aided the doctor in Corey's delivery, who was ready to enter the world with his face down instead of face up. The hospital staff was burdened that night with an abundance of deliveries. So much so, that there weren't enough recovery rooms or nursery cribs. Corey's delivery would require four hands, and it would have to be done quickly just prior to the final pelvic pushes. I was not worried and left all care in the hands of my Divine Master and loving God. All went well! Happiness and relief were the emotions drawn when Corey, my bundle of pure joy, was placed in my arms. This super-great moment of happiness was briefly interrupted with the sadness and anger I had against my mother for not being at my hospital bedside to greet her new grandchild. I was robbed of that memory, and yet my sister Denise had the privilege and comfort of my mother's presence in the life of all of her children. Denise's intuitiveness was always on cue because she was always at my rescue. Never hearing me utter those thoughts, she flew to Texas as soon as she could. Her aide and company was a healing balm in this now new way of life for me, called motherhood.

As much as I wanted to be a mother and have children, I was not emotionally prepared, nor was I equipped with the right role models in my parents. Even though I was not an alcoholic, as the child of an alcoholic, I still modeled the negative behavior I saw in my mother. The one thing I could never handle was my mother's yelling. I made a promise when I was a teenager that I would never yell at my children. It was a promise that I would break over and over again.

I thought that I could prevent myself from becoming like my mother, so I abstained from all alcohol from the time I was 23 until I was 44 years old. In my thirties, I had been taught by legalistic doctrine that drinking any amount of alcohol was a sin. Many pastors preach and teach this because of the over-indulgent society in which we live. However, if we are instructed on how to live an obedient Christian lifestyle of moderation in everything we do, then we can comfortably preach and teach from the book of Ecclesiastes 9:7.

> *"Go, eat your food with gladness, and drink your wine with a joyful heart, for God has already approved what you do."*

It is not the alcohol that is sinful, it is the excessive drinking behavior that is harmful and sinful. The apostle Paul reminds us in *Ephesians 5:18.*

> *"Do not get drunk on wine, which leads to debauchery. Instead, be filled with the Spirit."*

Like so many people, my mother let the woes of her life entrap her into a dark depressed world of habitual intoxication.

> *"Be careful, or your hearts will be weighed down with dissipation, drunkenness and the anxieties of life, and that day will close on you unexpectedly like a trap."*

> —LUKE 21:34

My mother's heavy heart did not afford me enough positive lessons to glean from her motherhood. Even with this acknowledgment I cannot blame my mother for my parenting flaws. I own the fact that my three children reaped the negative benefits of my frustration, anger, impatience and…yelling. I had my own share of demons that kept me in bondage.

Yet, I loved the idea of bringing a life into the world that I would love, cherish and train up as God would have me to do. Jeffrey and I would give our children a solid home environment. At first it seemed like all would be well with motherhood and my firstborn. I had only six weeks maternity leave from work so I made the very best of my new motherhood. I showered my firstborn with so much love. I enjoyed the daily and weekly routines of work, church, and motherhood, juggling the usual things that working moms and wives must manage. However, a year later, I wanted to stay home and be with my son. I was well aware that money was already tight, yet I was willing to make the sacrifice. There was something blissful about being with my baby, enjoying the little things with him, and just being near him. It was a brief two years that seemed like a day when I had to return to work. Our couple arguments now centered on money. Three years later, the finances got better and we decided to work on our second child. I was eight months pregnant when Jeffrey accepted a great job in Massachusetts. The birth of Janay was another phenomenal moment in my life, and again I missed my mother's presence especially when Janay arrived home. She was a colic newborn. Three hours at a time she would cry, day and night; the pediatrician attributed it to gas build up after she nursed. The only cure was time, by which her body would grow and be able to properly digest the milk. That time came when she was about three months old. Corey was such a big help for a four year old, getting me diapers, pacifier, and anything else I needed. He was smart and I enjoyed his company, except when I was tired or busy cleaning. I was sleep-deprived and had no energy. It was too much for me to handle. I was not able to give Corey the attention he needed and I grew more and more impatient with him. When he would ask me a question, I would give him a firm answer with a tone that said don't bother me. If he misbehaved, I would first yell and then ask him what happened. In those moments after, I felt I had betrayed him as a mother, each time promising myself that I would never raise my voice to him like that. It was a wonderful intention that never materialized. When my last baby was born it would be ten years apart from my daughter's birth. The pregnancy was a surprise. Once we got over the shock, we anticipated his birth, with marvelous excitement just as if it had been our first birth. The night Blair was born, his siblings, dad and my dear friend Brenda, were all in the delivery room, as part of his birth. Unfortunately, my impatience and harshness carried into his life. "Hurry, let's go, don't make me wait" rang loud in all of the lives of my children. If they were lacking or irresponsible with chores or school work, I first yelled at the very top of my voice. My emotions would always get out of control, usually making mountains out of mole hills. I did not know how to let the little things go, and to pray over the big things. I was a mess of a mother, and I knew it. I would ask God forgiveness and ask for help. I would study God's word in Galatians 5:22-23 on the fruit of the spirit.

> "But the fruit of the Spirit is love, joy, peace, forbearance,
> kindness, goodness, faithfulness, gentleness and self-control."

I especially prayed for self-control. I just knew that I would do better. But, each time I failed the test, and the cycle would be repeated. Just like an addiction, I would behave badly, yell or be quick with them, say words that I would regret, then feel guilt, and feel remorseful until the next time.

One of the hardest, most painful confessions is the admission of being a bad parent. Did I teach my children their prayers? Did I kiss them goodnight and read them bedtime stories? Did I cook healthy yet tasty meals? Did I keep the house sparkling clean? Did I teach them that Jesus was their best friend? Did I teach them to be well-mannered? Did I teach them how to count and say the alphabet? Did I go out of my way to get the best supplies for their school projects? Did I attend every one of their teacher/parent conferences? Did I spend countless hours reviewing school work and preparing my children for their school tests? Did I make every one of their school performances or sport's games? Did I wipe their tears away when they fell down or got bullied? Did I console them when racism blindsided them? Did I tell them that I love them? *Yes to all of them.* Did I do my best to make sure they were emotionally safe? *No, I did not.* This one negative almost derails all of my other positive parental provisions. I say almost because the positive is not to be dismissed; however, the positive is certainly overshadowed by my negative attributes as a mother. What does it mean that my children were not emotionally safe? It means that I created an environment that made it very hard for them as children and teen agers to speak what was on their mind. They had grown up with me reactively responding…reacting first, before thinking. I did not know how to be a calming presence. Since I had to grow up quickly and be prepared for life, I thought the same for my children. I had a countenance of expediency…things had to be done, now, not the next five minutes; if not, my patience was shot and I would come at them with my voice.

My patience and yelling was not just at the children, but also, my husband. I did not realize that my present life frustrations and challenges were being filtered by my past hurts and disappoint-ments. As my children got into their adolescent years, I did not physically embrace or hug them as frequently as I had done when they were younger. Each day I had given them a big hug when they left and returned from school. As they got older, my fear of rejection surfaced. I was stuck in my rejection. I had believed that they would not want my affection. I had also convinced myself that in between my apologies, they had grown upset with me. My fear of rejection prevented me from taking the risk. I should have just continued hugging them and asking them how they felt about my affection. As easy as it sounds now, it was something I did not want to acknowledge or confront. The brunt of my past would be inflicted on the ones that were the closest to me, the ones that I loved so very much.

Most of my life since a teenager, I strived to move onto something or somewhere better, steadfast in my head, that movement was my answer away from my past onto a more perfect future. It never occurred to me to be still and to think about my past.

"Be still before the Lord and wait patiently for him…Refrain from anger and turn from wrath; do not fret—it leads to evil."

—Psalm 37:7-8

I did not take time to think about why I was often angry. Why I was impatient? Why when my children got to the age of twelve, did I not hug them as much as when they were younger? Why did I take almost every word that someone said so personally? Why was movement so important to me?

Movement had become my false refuge. The movement in my reality was stagnant. I was going nowhere. I was stuck in the past with my five long lost friends…chaos, fear, alcohol, abandonment, and anger. I had become a pillar of salt. I just did not know it.

CHAPTER SEVEN

GETTING UNSTUCK

She is clothed with strength and dignity;

—Proverbs 31:25

A Virtuous Bouquet

A woman of God, rich in God's goodness, tells her story
so others may be blessed and share her victory!
Her smile brings a contagious joy and
her words of counsel penetrate the souls of many.
Plenty and versatile is her wisdom,
Enough to fill the pages of several books.
She is a morning glory that rises early...

Her daily schedule entwined with domestic
Responsibility and kingdom labor, fills her twenty-four hours to the brim.
Yet her radiance seems to never waiver.
Weary she may be, her anointing continues like a river...
always there, but always moving.
She is a sunflower that beams through the days of her brilliance...

Her husband is respected at the city gates where he takes his seat among
the elders. He praises her with all love and integrity.
Her children call her blessed. And blessed she is, with the beauty
that comes from very deep within her core.
Her love for others is a sincere conviction.
She is a rose to cherish and adore...

I penned this poem in 1999 for a mothers' and wives' ministry, not realizing that those words that birthed out of Proverbs 31 were words into the window of my future. Thirty years prior was my physical birth. Sixteen years prior had been my spiritual birth, the time when I had accepted Jesus as my Lord and as my Savior. Yet, even in being spiritually born again, I was emotionally still stuck. I prayed. I read scripture. I went to Christian workshops. I read Christian self-improvement books. I just knew that I had all of the information necessary for me to fix myself. The problem was that I was only looking at the surface symptoms. It was like trying to fix a leaky roof by patching several shingles; a repair that works well for a small leak on a brand new roof. But, if the roof has had a few layers of shingles added over the years, patching the top layer is futile. Most likely, a new roof is the only answer. The water that had trickled in from my past over the years had caused leaks that were not obvious to me. As the years transpired, these subtle leaks caused severe damage. The water gradually seeped through all of the layers and into the wood frame resulting in rot and mildew. If ignored, untreated and not fixed with a new roof, the damage would eventually infiltrate the foundation. The small leaks would pile into big puddles between the ceiling and roof, causing a stress that would ultimately burst with flooding. This is what was occurring in my life internally. I had harbored anger, bitterness and unforgiveness. When triggers were activated, I would burst with anger. Emotional triggers are events or people that consistently set off intense, emotional reactions within an individual. Most of the time, triggers occur without the person recognizing the original source.

I ignored the leaks in my foundation because I did not know or see them and I had no idea where they had originated. I was patching the top surface never getting to the rot and mildew. I repeatedly asked myself why was I not getting better. Why was I still clinging onto bitterness and anger? It would be another eleven years before I got the answer. During those in-between years, making vain attempts at patching my emotional leaks, I had become seriously intrigued with the Bible and joined various bible study groups in and out of my church. I especially desired to learn more about the persons and stories of the Old Testament. I developed a hunger for knowledge of the language that God spoke to his people. This quest for Hebrew and then Greek put me in a space of reflection. I reached out to God and asked him how would I gain this knowledge? God told me to attend seminary. That very next fall in 2003, I began my seminary journey at Pittsburgh Theological Seminary. It was difficult and ever so stressful to juggle three children, one 'foster' teen, a full-time job and an intense part-time coursework. My usual study hours were between 10 p.m.–12 midnight or 3 a.m. to 6 a.m. Time, money and pressure escalated the stress level in our home and I became more frustrated with my children and with my husband. The light at the end of the tunnel got dimmer when after my husband was laid off. I quit seminary until we moved from Pennsylvania to Massachusetts where he accepted a new job. Gordon-Conwell would be the next seminary until our next move to California, where I would attend Fuller Theological Seminary full-time.

When the Lord first commanded me to apply to seminary, I never imagined that it would be the place where God would begin his process of fixing me. I had always thought of divinity school as the place where I was to learn how to help others…how to minister to the needs of others. I found out that, before I could minister to others, I had to confront my own elephants head on. I had to embrace this little girl lost. God was directing my paths. His divine navigation system was in place, secured with global satellites set in the heavenly realms. Instead of calling it the Global Positioning System, I have named this GPS, God's Positioning Steps because every single step I took during those enduring seminary years was positioned for my own healing.

> *"In his heart a man plans his course, but the Lord determines his steps."*
>
> —PROVERBS 19:21

By no means was it an overnight miracle. It was a process of healing still in progress.

Seminary provided me a comprehensive academic education. I discovered the thrill and agony of transliteration and translation of Hebrew and Greek. I discovered the science and art of biblical exegesis and hermeneutics. I discovered biblical history, Christology, systematic theology, black theology, family counseling, pastoral care, and the theology of social justice. These were fantastic discoveries, yet none of these discoveries awakened my inner-core the way in which Clinical Pastoral Education (CPE) did. CPE was where I discovered my past, and began to find 'the little girl lost.'

CPE was a required course for all Master of Divinity students. Since I was not familiar with CPE, I made the assumption that it would be of no great use for me and delayed taking it until my last semester (God must have a phenomenal sense of humor.) CPE is a program of professional education for ministry. It is structured to provide clinical training for hospital, hospice and military *chaplains*, an experience that uses real–life ministry encounters. I soon found out that CPE was no ordinary course. One of the primary objectives of CPE is to develop students' *awareness* of themselves as ministers and of the way their ministry *affects persons*. In order to help and heal the emotional condition of a patient, we had to help and heal our emotional condition. Prior to stepping on any hospital unit floor, we students had to complete our first written assignment which was a paper 'telling our stories'. We were asked to include our family dynamics, our personal fears, challenges and life struggles... all things that I absolutely, positively and adamantly did not want to not put on paper and certainly not discuss within a group. That paper rekindled painful emotions of my personal history. It made me confront the sad truths that I had repressed, that I kept hidden in the deep recesses of my mind for so many years. The next step was even more frightening when it was my turn to read my story aloud becoming fully exposed...naked with the truth of my past. My pride would get the very best of me as I was preparing to be embarrassed showing my elephants. I did not want to appear weak, to appear the victim of circumstances. I could not shake the fact that I would be with this group eight hours a day for three months, and they would know my dark secrets. My privacy would be at stake for the sake of 'airing my dirty laundry'. I thought, black people just don't do this. A part of me believed that I was betraying my mother and father for this disclosure; guilt and fear rose up within me as I presented. I did not want to be judged, tried and condemned. I had experienced this condemnation years prior when I sought help and shared some of my past with pastors, pastor's wives and other Christian leaders within the church. Essentially, these leaders had not been formally educated to deal with pastoral care concerns. They would respond with insensitive comments, contrite sayings, or scripture throwing. Scripture throwing is when someone throws a scripture verse at you when they really do not know what to say. It is a safe way out for them, but leaves you, the one who came to seek help, emp-ty-handed. In those moments I would feel embarrassed and wonder why I bothered telling my business. As I waited my turn to present, I thought the same response would occur again, stirring up my very active imagination with great trepidation. All of this negative antici-pation went out the window when my supervisor started the session with how we were to proceed. She instructed us that the dialogue allowed after each story would be questions for clarification only if someone did not understand what was being said. Otherwise, there would be no conversation or random comments. She reinforced this emotionally safe environment by stating that every word of every story is confidential and never to be shared outside of the group. I was still a bit nervous when I presented, but once I felt the warmth in this group, I began to feel safe as I continued with my story. I had shed a few tears and noticed that a few of my peers did the same. There was no judgment or condemnation. I was now taking the first step of getting unstuck…I was *acknowledging my past.*

After I presented my story to the CPE group, I observed that although no one had my story, each person had a story; they were just carrying different baggage. I realized that almost every-one has some kind of elephant they grew up with. A bond had been created among us as we listened empathically to each oth-er's pain. I learned another great discovery. It was the difference between sympathy and empathy. Sympathy is having a mutual understanding or experience, having an affinity with the persons' circumstance. For instance, you tell me that your mother died and I respond, "I'm so sorry, I know how you feel, my mother died." What usually happens next, is that the person who said "I'm sorry continues with their experience talking forever about their mother, hardly giving you, the one who is in need of consoling, a chance to continue. You then leave as you entered, without any consolation. Empathy is identifying and understanding a person's circumstance. When a person is empathic, she is imagining what it is like walking in the other person's shoes, not their shoes. An empathic listener is an active listener responding when necessary to demonstrate that she is *hearing* and *feeling your pain*.

CPE opened a whole new world of trust for me. The reason is not magical or mystical, it is simple. I was in an *emotionally safe environment*, where trust lived. I applaud my CPE supervisor who set the tone with the following rules of engagement:

WHEN GIVING FEEDBACK...

- Be sure you are invited to offer feedback and that the other person is receptive.

- Be sure of your motivation. Help the other person's process and avoid trying to prove yourself right by being condescending.

- Be sure that you are understood. Ask the other person if they understood your feedback.

WHEN RECEIVING FEEDBACK...

- Be sure to check for understanding of what has been said. When the giver's intention is clear, the receiver will be likely to feel less defensive.

- Be sure to acknowledge the giver's feelings. Be sensitive to what you see and hear.

- As the receiver, be sure to offer your own reactions to feedback. If you, the receiver don't share any reaction (verbal or non-verbal), then the giver doesn't know where she stands with the receiver and she is less likely to risk offering feedback in the future.

The most valuable gift given to me was the gift of confidentiality, knowing that what was said would never be repeated outside of the group. In my ministry practice, I have set the same standards regarding confidentiality in personal counseling sessions and in group settings. Unfortunately, within our personal relationships and church fellowships, we have become increasingly reckless with people's personal business. Time and time again, numerous women have approached me at the conclusion of my workshop or sermon, stating that their trust has been scarred because someone betrayed their confidence. Sadly, some of this broken trust occurred through prayer or bible study with someone saying, "Let's pray for Betty and her husband." I have often reminded folks that using prayer as vehicle to expose someone's pain or vulnerability without their permission is gossiping. Gossiping is ugly and sinful. James 3:5-6 addresses the power of the tongue and its capacity for damage.

> *"So too the tongue is a small part of the body, yet it has great pretensions. Think how small a flame sets a huge forest ablaze. And the tongue is a fire! The tongue represents the world of wrongdoing among the parts of our bodies. It pollutes the entire body and sets fire to the course of human existence— and is set on fire by hell."*
>
> —NET

We women must get better with our tongues and know when to keep our mouths shut. When we do speak we should use our tongue carefully and with discretion, and protect a person's confidentiality that has been entrusted to us. Trust is a priceless treasure.

The day I told my story to my peers was only the tip of the iceberg in my personal and clinical pastoral journey. Patient visits, patient encounters, or clinical patient visits are terms used in CPE when on the various hospital units or floors. That next week we were on the floors to put our ministry to work. I just knew I was prepared, since I had twenty-eight years of ministry experience, three years professionally working with cancer patients and families, and three years professionally working with addicted mothers. I was ready to be at the bedside of a patient, to comfort, to console, and to share encouraging words. But, my reality proved otherwise, when a male patient yelled at me and told me leave him alone. I was *offended*, and *resented* this patient for his meanness when all I did was enter his room with a smile and kind voice. Why was he so upset *with me*? What in the world *did I do* to him to deserve this treatment? I left that room feeling rejected which then quickly evolved into *a quiet anger* which then turned into 'an attitude'. I thought how dare he treat me like this? By the time I got to my CPE session I was ready to unload my experience and get sympathy and empathy. This expectation was quickly shattered when my CPE supervisor threw a 90 mile-per-hour curve ball at my patient encounter experience. It was my wake-up call to my past. She asked me the following questions: "Why did you feel rejected? What made me feel angry? Why do you think he was upset with you? Why do you think you did something to him? I was unaware that these questions were the keys to the locked doors of my past and in that moment I was only *capable* of providing *surface answers*. Here is how I responded. "I felt rejected because the patient did not let me stay with him and did not want my help. I became angry because he rejected me. He must have gotten upset because he did not like me because I was black, because I was a woman." I did not know how to answer her last question, "Why did you think you did something to him?" A CPE supervisor always asks a question for a specific reason. She knew I could not *yet* answer that question on my own. She offered me the many possible reasons why that patient dismissed me. She stated that the patient could have been in pain or some kind of physical or emotional discomfort when I entered into his circumstance and that his response could have had absolutely nothing to do with me. That was easy to accept and to listen to. The next part would be extremely difficult to swallow when my supervisor returned to my surface answers. She asked, "Why was your immediate response to feel rejected?" Could this have something to do with feeling rejected as a child? My immediate response went into defense mode. In my head I was having a tantrum and trying to figure out how to get out of that room. I was thinking I did not sign up for this! Then I remembered that I was in a safe place. My defense went down and I chose to be part of the group process even if it would take me to places emotionally that I did not want to go. I went back to my childhood and thought about the experiences that had involved rejection. I remembered the times I was rejected because of my skin color from blacks and whites. I remembered feeling rejected whenever I was the third wheel amongst children my age, never experiencing being a best friend, like other kids I knew. I then thought of my father's absence, his negligence, as well as my mother's carelessness in making alcohol the priority over me. My emotional welfare as a child had been neglected. Many children believe that in some way that they are a part of the problem and to some degree I thought that I was responsible for their worries which ended in arguments. This childhood loaded with rejection and abandonment is what really made me feel rejected, offended and angry when the male patient yelled and dismissed me. I thought that maybe it was my skin color, or maybe I did something to that patient to cause him to get upset, just like I thought I did something to cause my parents to verbally fight over bills, drinking and gambling. Clearly, my parent's issues had nothing to do with me; in the same manner whatever that patient was going through, had nothing to do with me. As hard as it was to get this stuff out and speak to it; it was amazing! I was now able to answer my supervisor's questions with a meaningful and relative reply. She told me that if I was willing to go deep and be completely open and honest with myself, that I would grow beyond my expectations. She further mentioned that what I put into the CPE process is what I will get out of it. Her words gave me clarity. I was able to identify why I wore my feelings on my sleeve. I could now understand why I would react defensively, sometimes becoming an emotional wreck if my husband, children or others would say certain things or not give me the attention that I believed I deserved. In my mind it was a form of rejection, something I feared.

Retrospection is the act or process of surveying the past. Over the years since my CPE experience, I have thought about the steps it took for me to move toward my healing and to explore what it meant getting unstuck. The process involved 5 Steps:

- Acknowledging

- Confronting

- Embracing

- Releasing

- Moving Forward

Sharing my story the first day of CPE and then going deep, and being honest about my childhood in that patient encounter, allowed me to step into my past and acknowledge it. I was no longer keeping it hidden way down deep never to be thought of or mentioned. I was coming out of the dark and into the light of my past. This first step positioned me to take the next step. At the end of this chapter and the next five chapters, you will be challenged and guided through these steps. If you are willing to take the challenge, be honest and be willing to open your mind and heart so you can move beyond any possible fears, and put in to the process what you want to get out of the process, then I promise that you will gain more than your expectations! Put your heart and trust in the one who knows you best and loves you more than yourself—God your heavenly creator.

> *"...in all things we are more than conquerors through him who loved us. For I am convinced that neither death nor life, neither angels nor demons, neither the present nor the future, nor any powers, neither height nor depth, nor anything else in all creation, will be able to separate us from the love of God that is in Christ Jesus our Lord."*
>
> —ROMANS 8:37-39

GETTING UNSTUCK STEP BY STEP

STEP 1: ACKNOWLEDGING YOUR PAST

Ignorance can keep you weak and in the dark whereby knowledge is powerful and brings light. Before you can get unstuck, you must know what has you stuck. Digging deep into our memories can be almost as painful as the actual experience. The emotions will rise up and the tears will fall once you dig up the pain. Don't stop because it hurts. Continue because it does hurt so you can keep moving. Don't fight the hurt. It has to come out. Trust the process: Begin by writing your story and then reading your story aloud. Here are some suggested elements in:

Unveiling Your Story

- **THINK** about your childhood, your parents, siblings, other family members.

- **REMEMBER** your feelings as a child, teen, and young adult.

- **IMAGINE** yourself a child.

- **DESCRIBE** your family and how those relationships impacted you and formed you.

- **REWIND** the tapes in your head and let them repeat.

- **WRITE** the impactful emotional events and turning points in your life.

- **WRITE** the relationships with others and how positively or negatively you were affected by: family, friends, mentors, pastors, co-workers, bosses, etc.

- **WRITE** your experience of God. Was God included in your world at that time? If yes, how? If no, what did it mean to your life experience?

- **COLLECT** 2-5 photographs and objects of the time in your life that caused pain. (include childhood) Keep them with you as you write. The more you see them the less it hurts to see them, to acknowledge them.

Make quiet alone time to write with **absolutely no disturbances**. *If the pain is too much to write the story in one session, then come back to it and continue. Give yourself a weekend or full work week to complete. Make a deadline, otherwise you will put it down and tuck it away.* **Remember**, *if you tuck it away, and keep putting it off, you are keeping yourself* **stuck in the past**.

When you complete your story, **first** *read it aloud to yourself, then think about who you would like to read aloud and unveil your story to. You need a person who you trust, who can hear your story and be non-judgmental, who can be okay with your tears and sadness, and not tell you to stop crying. You need someone who can be empathic not sympathetic. (You may have to explain to them what that means.)* **Pray to God** *who this person should be. The goal is to just acknowledge your past, unveil your past, to be able to tell someone your past, and to feel those emotions you had at that time. (fear, rejection, loneliness, abandonment, shame, dirty, being belittled, neglect, joy, laughter, sadness, anger, resentment, confusion, encouragement, anguish, discouragement...)*

As you move through this process hold onto God's hand, you are not alone.

> *"The Lord your God is with you...He will take great delight in you, he will quiet you with his love,"*
>
> —Zephaniah 3:17

CHAPTER EIGHT

FORGIVE, BUT NEVER FORGET

*For if you forgive others when they sin against you, your
heavenly Father will also forgive you. But if you do not
forgive others their sins, your Father will not forgive your sins*

—Matthew 6:14

Love letter to my unborn first born

I have wondered what you would have become, a scientist, a poet?
Who knows?
Would you have been tall or short?
I wonder if you would have looked like your brothers or your sister?
Who knows?
You would have been my first born. But I never gave you the chance to be…
a storyteller, a savvy politician, or maybe a preacher
Who knows?
You would have been my first born. But you were an inconvenience.
I never gave you the chance to be…
my blessing, my pride and joy.
I have asked God to forgive me, and I have that peace within my

soul. Yet I still wonder what you would have become
if I had given you the chance to be...
my first born.
We have never touched as mother and child.
I never held you or smelled your newborn scent.
Forgive me for not giving you the chance to be...
my first born.
I know that love transcends and is eternal.
I believe in my heart that our resurrected souls will one day connect again
me as your mother and you as
my first born.

The phrase, "forgive and forget is not in the bible. It is usually used figuratively, for we human creatures do not have the mental capacity to forget the sins of our transgressors the way God forgives.

> *"For I will forgive their wickedness and will remember their*
> *sins no more."*

—HEBREWS 8:12

The scripture does not require us to forget when we forgive a person; it instructs us to forgive from the heart graciously the way Jesus forgives us.

> *"Be kind and compassionate to one another, forgiving each*
> *other, just as in Christ God forgave you."*

—EPHESIANS 4:32

Xarízomai (Charizomai) is the Greek word in this verse that means forgiving. It literally means to exercise *grace, freely,* show *favor.* Its root is xaris which means grace, willing and freely extending favor, to bestow unconditionally. Forgiveness means to extend grace and favor, and to unconditionally pardon someone the remission of penalty exonerating and excusing a person's sin against you. It is an act of one's will, a purposeful decision. A conscious exertion accompanied by deep thought comprises a person's intention to forgive another person. Although God requires us to forgive, it is not easy, and the choice is ultimately up to us to decide. What holds us back from forgiving someone? Feelings. Hate, fear, bitterness, anger, pride, rejection, sadness, and depression are major culprits in delaying forgiveness.

Prayer is the power that can help you move more swiftly to forgiving someone, because the benefits outweigh the feelings. Joy and peace are waiting for you once you have forgiven. You will have peace knowing that this deed is finally done! You will experience pure joy knowing that you have pleased God!

When God forgave me quickly and without hesitation, I knew that I had to graciously and without any conditions, do the same. I had to forgive those whom I thought did not deserve my forgiveness. But who am I to think that? I am just as undeserving, yet God forgave me. I had wanted to suppress the terrible act of abortion. It was a sin against God, and against my unborn baby. I am glad that I did not forget this act because I would not have asked God's forgiveness and I would have never forgiven myself. Instead, I am relieved and so very blessed that I gave this burden to my Lord, Jesus.

"My guilt has overwhelmed me like a burden too heavy to bear."

—*Psalm 38:4*

I no longer walked with the shame and guilt, hoping that the world would never know my dark secret. *Kept secrets keep you stuck.*

In 1983 when I gave this part of my past to God, I told God that I would use this as a testimony to help other women rid their lives of shame and guilt. God afforded me that opportunity in 2006, when he birthed the O.A.S.I.S 139 (Offering Affirmation Spiritually in Self-Expression, Psalm 139) ministry into my Spirit. I was not a minister or pastor. I was a servant in the church willing to do what God asked of me. However, this opportunity did not come until eighteen years later. God knew that prior to this, I was not yet ready. Deep down, I knew the same. O.A.S.I.S 139 was a ministry that allowed women to come together in an emotionally safe setting where they could creatively express their pains, their hurts and their struggles. This particular event was open to the public, inviting women to listen or to share their testimony through song, spoken word, musical instruments, or canvass painting. It was that evening on stage, at a community center auditorium where for the first time, I read my poem, *Love letter to My Unborn Firstborn*. God had prepared me to be ready for that moment to be a blessing to those who were emotionally hurt. Women gave testimonies about being raped, abused and unloved. Many of the women were not affiliated with any church, yet stated how they felt the presence of God in that place. Some shared their pain and some did not, and that was okay. Sometimes people want to jump right in to tell the world about their story. God works differently with each one of his children. Your time may not be my time, and my time may not be your time. So when is it the right time? You will know when you have been liberated, and when God opens the door of opportunity. Take it to God in prayer. In the meanwhile, work on the rest of your healing.

Acknowledge your entire past, and then confront your entire past. Acknowledging my past was indeed a milestone for me. It opened my eyes to recognize my pain. I was outside looking into the windows of my childhood, looking in at the painful experiences, seeing how they affected me, watching how I reacted, and feeling the hurt all over again. The open window revealed who I was at that time. I was vulnerable, insecure, alone, and lost. Acknowledging my past meant the self-admission of my deep-rooted pain that had wounded me for so many years. Acknowledging my past meant that I could transition into confronting my past and see myself up close, face to face. I would now hold up the mirror and see what had become of that little girl lost.

If you keep your past pushed so far down where you cannot touch it, see it or remember it, then it has become forgotten. If it is forgotten, you will never learn from your past, never finding the courage to confront your past or to deal with your complicated persona. You will never find the courage to forgive and to be forgiven. You will not be aware of your emotional triggers that will continue to rise up. Triggers are sneaky and you will not see them coming, nor will you understand why you are reacting the way you do. Confronting your past reveals your strengths, weaknesses and limitations. You can create a checks and balance awareness journal to self-evaluate how you are doing at handling the hard stuff you are confronting. Two of the most challenging areas in confronting ones past are triggers and forgiveness. They are most difficult because they involve relationships. A range of emotions can surface when a person is triggered. Insecurity, jealousy, frustration, defensiveness, and anger is the short list of possible triggers. The way a person copes with these triggers could come in the form of silence, emotional outbursts, or passive/aggressiveness. None of these are good coping mechanisms and have great potential to damage and even ruin relationships. If you stay in the dark with your past, your past can get in the way of your present and future.

I was in the dark with my past for too long, never caring to acknowledge it. I had no clue what emotional triggers were or how much they negatively impacted my life. I saw myself as a sensitive, kind, caring, loving lamb, concerned about others. My husband, children, and telemarketers saw me as an aggressive, defensive, angry, roaring and wounded lion. How could these two very different perspectives exist? This duality existed due to the emotional triggers set in my past. On more than one occasion my husband would refer to me as Dr. Jekyll and Mr. Hyde. I can chuckle now, but when he would say this, it would get me more upset because I did not see myself in that way, except when I became provoked and then frustrated. Criticism was difficult for me to digest because it signified that I failed or was incomplete. My initial response to criticism would usually be defensive, making every effort to justify my performance. Another reaction would occur if I thought I was not being heard, understood, or having things my way. My childhood feelings of insecurity and rejection would be triggered resulting in my negative coping mechanisms. I would get angry and raise my voice to yelling. It was my way of being heard and being in control. But it never worked; I never got the results I had wanted. Instead, these coping mechanisms pushed them away, inciting my feelings of abandonment. This emotional trigger would bring feelings of sadness. After crying, I reacted with silence and reclusion as my protective gear to withdraw while simultaneously desiring sympathy. Like my other negative coping mechanisms, I never got what I sought after these tantrum episodes. It was like I was six years old sitting alone dealing with my world, the only way I knew how.

I had been ignorant and blind until years later, when CPE encouraged me to confront my past, providing me with the self-awareness and understanding I needed to confront my emotional triggers. In case you are wondering, triggers do not go away over night; instead, they appear to fade away as you become better at recognizing them and identifying them. I work on identifying them each time. I do mean work. When a trigger does surface, I ask myself, "Why am I getting frustrated? Why am I so upset? Am I reacting from a place in my past or am I responding in the present?" Asking these questions allows me time to cope positively. As you continue on this journey be mindful that your improvement may not be recognized by those who have been impacted by your negative coping mechanisms. Do not let that discourage you. It may hurt you at first, but as you continue to confront your stuff, the good and the bad, you will own up to your flaws and take responsibility.

> *"When I was a child, I talked like a child, I thought like a child, I reasoned like a child. When I became a man, I put away childish ways behind me."*
>
> —I CORINTHIANS 13:11

Do not quit when it gets hard, getting through the hard stuff pays off. Every bit counts toward your victory! Confronting my past was the yucky part of getting unstuck. Admitting how emotionally ugly I could and can be with my precious family saddens me. It is not pretty looking in the mirror seeing the lion. But the more I face that lion head-on, the more it will fade away, and the lamb will be in full view. So too it will be for you as you continue looking in the mirror.

Identifying my triggers incited me to examine why I reacted so intensely when those feelings of rejection, insecurity and abandonment surfaced, and why was I always needing to be in control. These questions led me to my parents and to my older brother. The issue of forgiveness was something I would now confront. It required another hard look in the mirror. I had to completely forgive my parents and my older brother. I also had to ask forgiveness from my husband, children and from God.

The next question for me was, "How was I to forgive the dead?" When I looked at the scriptures on forgiving, they encompassed the act of bestowing grace and pardon. Earlier in this chapter I mentioned that forgiveness was a gesture that came from the heart and was an act of unmerited kindness. It did not matter that my parents and brother were dead because the bitterness and repressed feelings were very much alive in me and I was holding on to their memories ungraciously. The memories were also tearing me apart from my true self. The festering inside had to cease.

I blamed my mother for so many things in my life. She did not protect my tender feelings when I caught her attempted suicide even though I was too young to understand. Yet the visual is still very vivid. History repeated itself when I was fourteen and caught her in that same position. Whether she was merely crying for help or had serious intentions, the image for the second time was stamped into my memory. My mother was not emotionally available to me when I needed her the most throughout my childhood and teen years. When she died, I resented her for leaving me. She would not be at any of my special moments…graduation, marriage, the births of my children, my children's accomplishments, my twenty-fifth marriage renewal ceremony or my ordination. I had to tell myself to get over the visuals that scarred me and to get over the lost moments, or else I would stay stuck. All the bitterness and resentment in the world will never change what I saw, nor will it bring her back and return those lost moments I was never able to share with her as an adult. All that was now important, was for me to forgive, to graciously pardon her, and that is exactly what I did. In my heart, I believe if I had to forgive my mother in person we both would have shed tears and then embraced each other.

"Therefore, as God's chosen people, holy and dearly loved,
clothe yourselves with compassion, kindness, humility,

gentleness and patience. Bear with each other and forgive
whatever grievances you may have against one another.
Forgive as the Lord forgave you. And over all these virtues put
on love, which binds them all together in perfect unity."

—COL 3:12-13

Prior to my self-awareness, I frequently stated that I hate the father of my childhood and love the father of my adult years. My mother left my father when I was seven years old. My father made some attempt to see me but in my eyes never tried hard enough. He abandoned all of us with his absence and with his lack of support leaving my mother to struggle by herself raising us. He chose gambling over us. When I was fourteen I forgave my father. I did not know how to utter the words to him so I said them to myself. I forgave him for being absent but I still harbored resentment towards him for neglecting my mother. I hated watching her being exhausted and lonely and sad. I blamed him for that. I was nineteen in college when I introduced him to Jeffrey. Since that day my dad was very much a part of my life until he died. He never missed a major event. He attended my children's celebrations, he gave gifts, he gave his time and he gave lots of love. My dad was an amazing grandfather, father-in-law and father. If I had not forgiven him when I was fourteen, I would have missed experiencing the presence of a father that I had badly craved. But there was more work for me to do in this area. He had been dead two years when I got the revelation that forgiveness was still due. I had to remove the ill feeling and blame I had for him for causing my mother's pain. As much as I thought my father was the blame, it was not my place to point or to judge. That was God's area, not mine. So, I forgave my dad, and moved on, remembering him with nothing but happiness and a smile in my heart. I now love the father of my childhood.

My big brother Tony was someone I had adored and looked up to until he put his hands around my throat. I lived in fear in his presence from that moment on. I could never fully understand how he could harm me in that way. I left one of the best schools in Boston because of him. I had blamed him for bringing more darkness into our lives. Years later, when we were together at family gatherings, I treated Tony as if nothing had happened. I loved him and missed the Tony of my younger years before he went dark. I had repressed those feelings of blame. It would be several years after his death when I would look in the mirror of my past, confront my feelings, then admit that I needed to forgive him. I released my feelings of blame giving them to God to be forever removed from my heart so could I make room for the wonderful Tony memories.

I would also have to ask forgiveness from my husband. Jeffrey was and still is the very best thing that has happened to me. I had longed for a love like his. My relationships with older males prior to him had been under the influence of my need to fill the father void. I had not experienced my father's love long enough to know what that looked like. Jeffrey truly loved me and I loved him. I just did not know how to love and love completely because of my fears and because of my anger. Most of the time, I responded to him from places in my past. There were times during our arguments he would ask me why I was reacting that way. I would go to my defense mode because I really did not know why. I did not have the self-awareness to identify my over-reactiveness. Jeffrey and I entered our marriage with loaded baggage. Although we had exchanged the stories of our childhood, our losses, and family secrets, we did not know what to do with the pain. So we exchanged our wedding vows convinced that the past would stay tucked away as we began our new lives together.

The past never stays tucked away. It enters our lives the way an electrical fire does. You do not see it coming and you cannot see the smoke because it is within the walls. You have no idea that there is fire burning beneath the surface ready to consume you. Your unresolved past works gradually and silently, infiltrating the walls of your present, consuming your relationships, burning your dreams and your hopes. Jeffrey meant the world to me, but I took him for granted. I could only see his flaws and imperfections. I would have to ask forgiveness. I did, and he forgave me, expressing his appreciation for my humility and honesty. As we continue in our marriage journey, we stay committed to our wedding vow, 'to possess a genuine trust in you'. Love is a given. Trust has to be nurtured before the time you say "I do." Jeffrey has been my knight in shining armor. He is a faithful man learning more and more to put his trust in God every day. His strength and wisdom have kept me and his children safe and secure. He has worked diligently and selflessly all these years to provide a financially stable home, always loving his family and making his family his number one priority. Jeffrey is my true love. I thank God for joining us together, and for keeping us together for 33 years. We have come this far by faith.

"…the righteous will live by faith."

—Romans 1:17

The risk of rejection has been a colossal obstacle for me in asking forgiveness from my children. My fear comes from the guilt I have for letting them down. They have witnessed the lion side of me more often than I would ever want to admit. I have projected my past on them with some of the same behavior that I modeled from my mother. Over the years I have apologized to my children when I have wronged them. However, I have not faced them directly and asked for their forgiveness. Denial has also been a cause in my delay, due to this shameful admission. I love them unconditionally and am thankful to God that he gave each of them to me. Corey, Janay and Blair are special having a unique place in my heart. I am so proud of their accomplishments, who they are striving to be and the adults that they have become. I will move beyond my denial and ask their forgiveness because it is too important to them... and to me. It is worth the risk, and I know that once I step out in love and just do it, I will be blessed with a great peace. As I stated previously, confronting your past is hard and requires endurance. Put your mind and heart to it. God will do the rest.

"I can do all things through Christ who strengthens me."

—PHILIPPIANS 4:13, NKJV

There have been many instances in my life when I projected my anger towards God. I cried out to Him angry that he had given me parents and a household full of chaos and dysfunction. Why couldn't I have had a normal childhood and a good life? I asked him why I was birthed into such an environment. Why did I have to see and experience so much pain, so much sorrow? I had hated the life I had been given. I finally gave up the anger and went to God asking forgiveness. I decided to accept that God had his reason and purpose for my life. As I am writing this for you, I see some of why God gave me the life I lived. He gave me it so that my life could help you with your life. I have no regrets.

GETTING UNSTUCK STEP BY STEP

STEP 2: CONFRONTING YOUR PAST

Confronting your past can be overwhelming and full of anxiety and a lot of work. So roll up your sleeves and get to work. There are many obstacles that can get in the way of you moving ahead.

The following will help get you through:

- **LOOK** into the mirror of your past and write how you behaved when you *were* emotionally hurt

- **WHAT** *feelings* did you experience? Those feelings are most likely your emotional triggers.

- **IDENTIFY** these *triggers.*

- **WRITE** them down.

- **WHEN** do you experience these triggers?

- **WHAT** are you *coping mechanisms* to these triggers? Are they *Negative or Positive?*

- **WRITE** them down.

How does your reaction impact those around you?

- **LOOK** in the mirror to see who you might have hurt by projecting your past pain on them through bitterness, anger envy, etc.

- **MAKE** *a list* of those you need to *ask forgiveness* and of those in your past that *you need* to *forgive.*

- **FORGIVE** person to person, if you have access to the individual.

Forgiveness is not always easy, yet it should not be delayed. Ask for God's help to get you to do it, and then do it.

- **WHAT** *obstacles* are in your way of forgiveness…whether to forgive or to be forgiven? Denial, shame, fear? **WRITE THEM DOWN**

*Forgiveness **does not always require** face to face encounters as in death or if a violent betrayal has caused severe emotional damage. Rape, molestation and physical abuse are some of these exceptions.*

Forgive but Never Forget.

When you have made the decision to forgive, it is to come from the heart graciously to pardon unconditionally. The act of forgiving is significant and transforming, and should never be forgotten.

CHAPTER NINE

GOD'S LOVE LETTER TO YOU

…I am fearfully and wonderfully made;
your works are wonderful,

—Psalm 139:14

Wonderful!

The wonders of God surround us
from the miniscule drop of dew to the magnificent ravishing redwood trees.
He is sovereign in rain storms, can you not hear the thunder?
He is ever powerful in the sun, can you not feel the heat?
Not a day goes by incomplete, did you watch the sun set?
Nor is a night mistaken, did you see the moon glow?
All is the perfect plan of our perfect Maker, God, our Creator
who thought each and every creature into existence,
the creature of land, the creature of air, the creature of sea
the creature you, and the creature me.
His majesty abounds in the air we breathe,
in the water we drink and on the grass we walk.
The Wonder of God must not be overlooked.

Oh my great and omnipotent God,
if we only paid more attention to the splendor of your wonder!
If we only took time to see you in your wonder!
If we only abided in the greatness of your wonder!
...then we could become wonderful!

Have you ever thought of yourself as wonderful? It is difficult and almost impossible to view yourself as wonderful when you are incomplete. When I wrote this in 2007, I did not feel or believe that I was wonderful. I was incomplete until I embraced my past. I still had a way to go in my healing process and self-awareness. I hated my past, which meant that I hated a part of me. I hated that lost little girl because it reminded me of the pain. I would have to learn how to love that little girl within me, the little girl of my past. Embracing my past was another key to that locked door. Embracing is accepting, cherishing, gladly welcoming, taking in, and including your past as part of your whole life. If I were to embrace my past, then I would have to embrace the little girl of my past. Embracing my past would mean for me to accept my pain while still loving the me in my past. How was I to do that? How was I to reclaim my past? I would reclaim my past by understanding the myths in my present life. These myths had been formed in my childhood and teen years marinating into my adulthood. Our mythology is built upon the convictions and beliefs that we have about ourselves, our relationships with others, and our roles at school, work, church and home. Reclaiming my past meant re-writing my myths. But first I would have to identify and name these myths.

During my CPE experience I discovered that I had six myths about myself: myth of sole responsibility/perfection, myth of rejection, myth of over-functioning, myth of self-sufficiency, myth of sacrificing joy and the myth of pleasing/self-sacrifice.

My *myth of sole responsibility and perfection* was rooted in my child-hood when roles became reversed between mother and daughter. My mother is what some might have called a 'functioning alcoholic' because she went to work every day, kept a clean house and kept her children fed and clothed. Functioning is a relative term since the question would be, how well or productive had she been in her functioning. Years later, as her drinking worsened, she would keep a bottle in her desk drawer at work. Because of my mother's work schedule, drinking and exhaustion, there were duties that she could not fulfil. My older brother had a job and was completing high school. So it was for me to fill the gaps, taking on adult responsi-bilities, and trying to be perfect in meeting those expectations. At eight and a half years old, my role included babysitter and tutor for my younger brother. After we walked home from school I would help him with his homework and get him a snack. By the time I was nine-years old, we had to take the subway train each day, to and from school. I loved my little brother Randall and did not want anything bad to happen to him. It was my responsibility to keep him safe as we made the half hour ride each way. I fell short of this responsibility two times; once when I lost him at the Boston Public Library; and once when he fell on a cement parking divider hitting his head hard enough to bleed. When the bleeding did not stop, I went to every retailer and hotel on that block until someone helped us. I did not call my mother until Randall was bandaged and the bleeding had stopped. The day I lost him in the library, I spent over an hour looking for him. I left afraid that he might have been hit by a car or taken by a stranger. During both of these crises, I blamed myself because I did not meet that perfect expectation, but instead failing in my responsibility. At the young age of nine I did not know any better. I was not informed that a nine-year old should not have those responsibilities and that a nine-year old is not emotionally equipped to handle that kind of pressure and burden.

Caring for my brother was one of many adult roles which I performed. I was therapist, cheerleader, and protector to my mother. When she got depressed, I made it my responsibility to try to cheer her up and to encourage her. In my teens, when she drank too much, I would hide her alcohol. When her boyfriend's mistress would call and harass her, I would come to her rescue, telling the women to never call our home again. When another of my mother's boyfriends became violent, I intervened by threatening to call the police. When my brother Tony got violent with my mother, I intervened to protect her.

The responsibility was a heavy burden for me, a child and teenager becoming prematurely an adult, making every attempt to meet those expectations with perfection. The myth of sole responsibility has caused my adulthood to suffer from an overblown sense of responsibility. The years that I worked for non-profit organizations and most of my years in ministry contained elements of this myth. Whether it was crack addicted pregnant mothers, cancer patients, vulnerable teens, or women with marriage issues, I went all out to ensure that I was doing all that I could do, and more, for them, still believing that I had not done enough, still believing that I had not lived up to my expectation of perfection. I operated in this mode as a mother micromanaging every detail of my children, not giving them the space to breathe. I wanted them to make only the right decisions to keep them from making mistakes, holding them to very high standards, with their cleaning chores, homework, sport and music lessons, college applications, and so on.

Most definitely, there is something good and positive in having high standards and striving to achieve high goals. This mentality turns sour when it is over-the-top. Being excessive is not good. Since I believed that I had to meet every expectation with perfection, I had that same expectation for others. Subconsciously, since I was convinced that I had to be perfect, I had the same expectation for my husband, my children, my staff, my co-workers and ministry leaders. When a person believes that she must be perfect or very close to it, she becomes consumed. She is always emotionally drained and frustrated simultaneously because she is striving to obtain the unobtainable. Being perfect is humanly impossible. I became a procrastinator because I did not want to start for fear of not meeting my expectation of perfection. I was stuck in my imperfect perfection of never being good enough. I was convinced that if I was perfect, then I would be accepted, never rejected.

The *myth of rejection* had significantly hindered my life. Having been emotionally neglected by my parents had permeated my being with the myth that I was not a priority. When I thought this, I would then experience feelings of rejection and abandonment. The myth of rejection was birthed in my childhood and teen relationships always being the third wheel. It taught me that I was never someone's priority. I was not accepted, believing that I was left out and abandoned. I felt these same feelings when I had dated older men and found out that they had other women while with me. As an adult, this myth caused my feelings to be super- sensitive when I believed or perceived that I was neglected and rejected, even when the reality was not so. This is fantasizing. I would make assumptions, creating and building them bigger, and interpret that circumstance as rejection. For example: if a female did not smile at me, then she must not like me; if my husband criticized me, I was not good enough and he rejected me; if my children forgot to get me Mother's Day cards, then I was not a good mother and they rejected me; if people did not remember and celebrate my birthday, I was not a good enough friend and would feel abandoned. The myth of rejection invokes a defensive position when acceptance is threatened, or even perceived as threatened. When in this defensive mode, I would react in three ways: I would withdraw like I was that little girl again and be alone; I could become angry and argumentative; or I could ignore it, which only caused more fantasizing and more assumptions about the person or situation. I had never had the courage to share my thoughts, to confront and ask questions directly. Confrontation is usually thought of as something bad due to the fact that a lot of folks do not know how to confront. Confrontation when done with the fruit of the spirit, with kindness and with goodness, can be a positive and productive encounter. I had not realized that then, and I refused risking being rejected again by confronting a person to get clarification. My myth of rejection had distorted my view and reasonability.

"Though seeing, they do not see;"

—MATTHEW 13:1

My *myth of self-sufficiency* taught me that I am independent and that I can manage everything myself. It had been ingrained since I was eight years old taking care of my brother, making sure that he did his homework after school before he went out to play, making peanut butter and jelly crackers for our snack and cleaning my room and the bathroom without ever being told. When I was in middle school, I would take my brother to wash clothes at the laundromat during the times that my mother was at one of her two jobs. If I needed something to wear before wash day, I would wash my clothes by hand and hang them on the radiator to dry.

I rarely asked my mother for help. I figured things on my own for two reasons. The first reason is that I did not want to disturb her and bring her more trouble and worry. The second reason is that when I needed money, I did not ask her because after food, utilities, rent, cigarettes and alcohol, there was nothing left. When she did run out of money and would ask me to borrow money from my friends' mother, it usually included money for her vices.

I would take her note to the liquor store where she had been a regular patron; the note stated that I was getting cigarettes for my mother. This was before it was unlawful to sell to minors. I despised this borrowing and buying, yet it had become routine. My myth of self-sufficiency taught me that if I needed things then I would have to get them. When I needed school clothes in middle school and high school, I worked the summers. When I needed a car to get to work in high school, I worked and saved the money on my own. When the university did not have a dorm room for me, I managed to get one by the end of that week. When I did not have enough work study money to pay for my college books and fees, I figured how to contact my father and ask him to help me. The good side of self-sufficiency is that I was able to think on my own and get what I needed to survive. The bad side of self-sufficiency is that I rarely acknowledged that I needed help, and when I did, I did not have any idea how to ask. I had conditionally operated from a place of independence, and had become accustomed to doing things my way. My way was the right way and the only way. If it was not done my way then it was wrong. The myth of self-sufficiency taught me that being in control eliminated chaos and confusion. I had to control my environment and control the people in it. A controlling person is a micromanager, a control freak, a person who has a very, very hard time swallowing criticism and coming out of denial. A control freak is also compulsive. My homes always had to be perfect looking like a model house with everything in its perfect place. Every bed was made, the kitchen and bathroom counter were absolutely spotless. Everything had to be in order. Nothing dirty was to ever be exposed.

When I identified my myth of self-sufficiency and understood how it had formed me, I was able to acknowledge it and confront it. I discovered that I no longer had to live in that survival mode. I no longer had to control my environment. I learned to give up this self-sufficiency mode. I learned that my way was not the only way, and eagerly considered different ideas and different methods. I worked toward taking down my guard to criticism. I worked toward asking and receiving help when I needed it. I embraced the notion that I did not have to be independent always relying solely upon myself, and that it was okay to depend on others. I embraced the idea that my world would not come down crashing into chaos if I let someone else be in control. I had to admit to myself that my compulsive independence kept me from relying on my heavenly Father…for everything, keeping me from my blessings and from my peace.

"Do not be anxious about anything, but in everything by prayer and petition, with thanksgiving, present your requests to God. And the peace of God which transcends all understanding, will guard your hearts and your minds in Christ Jesus."

—PHILIPPIANS 4:6–7

My *myth of over-functioning* worked hand in hand with my myth of self-sufficiency. I had believed that performing in this way was my role in achieving fulfillment in my life. I had believed that I was not productive or useful unless I was always busy: busy with cleaning, busy with projects, busy with church ministry and busy with helping everyone in the entire world. For many years, I was often too busy to pray or to study the bible. If I relaxed, read, or was sitting too long in one spot, I had to get up and do. Sitting, being still, or not helping someone meant that I was not being productive. This carried over into every area of my life. At church, I was involved with usually four to five ministries at once, believing that if there was a void, if there was an unfilled position, I would have to fill it, believing that it was my Christian responsibility. We may have several gifts that God has blessed us with, yet we do not have to use all of them at once. My myth of over-functioning convinced me that I was indispensable. I had to be taught that no one is indispensable, that I was not indispensable. I had to recognize that there is always someone better, and there is always someone to fill the gap, and I had to believe it. God has a way of bringing those gifted persons to the right place they need to be in the right role and at the right time.

I needed to stop trying to be superwoman. For me to do this, I would first have to get out of God's way and be still in the quiet of his presence. I had to settle into being more of a Mary and less of a Martha. For it was Mary who made time to anoint Jesus' feet in preparation of his coming death, while her sister Martha was busy with cooking and preparing the meal. Martha was doing a good thing but did not take a minute to see what was more significant in that minute and missed out on an opportunity of her lifetime. Having to always be busy is excessive and compulsive. I had been blinded to the negative consequences of over-functioning. I would regularly function on five hours of sleep a night juggling full-time work, children activities, homework, housework, cooking and church duties. During the day or weekends I hardly spent time on myself. Because of this personal neglect, I had a repressed resentment towards my family and church. Deep down, I had blamed them because my every waking minute was sacrificed for them. If I did not feel that they appreciated my sacrifice, I fantasized that they were ungrateful taking my sacrifice for granted. It was as if I thrived on negativity and on not being happy.

My *myth of sacrificing joy* kept my happiness at bay. Since I had not known how to be a child or how to enjoy being a child, I did not know how to completely open up to fun or frivolity. My childhood made me grow up prematurely. It was more important for me to be responsible than to have fun. That is how I survived as a child and teen. As an adult, my *myth of sacrificing joy* lied to me and had convinced me that having fun was a waste of time; especially when there were other things that had to be done. Fun could wait, responsibility could not.

When my children were in grade school they wanted me to be silly with them, or to play video games with them. My participation was usually brief or I said, "I can't right now." In my mind, there was always *something more important* like cleaning, preparing meals, or bible study lessons. If I did participate in fun, it was usually brief because I had to get to *something important.* I could always justify my behavior because I had the greatest reinforcement with my myth of sacrificing joy. My myth of sacrificing joy was always in my ear, reminding me that I was the one who kept things in order to eliminate chaos. I was the one who organized, planned and managed everything so that everyone else was cared for. I was the caregiver, and prided myself on taking a no-nonsense approach to every activity. My husband and children loved to joke and be frivolous. Most of those times I stayed busy. I either felt there was something important to do or I felt uncomfortable and awkward being silly. I felt that I did not fit in with their fun. As I looked in the mirror of this myth, I encountered the truth that none of those 'important' things were important enough to sacrifice my joy…to sacrifice some of the best quality time that I could have experienced with my family to cherish forever. I regret that I did not have the eyes to see that.

> *"A cheerful heart is good medicine, but a crushed spirit dries up the bones."*
>
> —PROVERBS 17:22

The *myth of pleasing and self-sacrificing* implies that an individual will sacrifice themselves to please at any cost. That was me, particularly with adult friends and my relationships at church and at work. I would drop what I was doing to help or care for someone else. If someone asked for help, I figured how to accommodate their needs even if it inconvenienced me or took a great deal of time. The act of pleasing came easy to me as a child of alcoholic parents. I wanted to please my mother so she would not have to worry about me. In a sense I was also enabling her drinking and behavior. The more independent I had become, the more comfortable she got with her drinking and emotional neglect. Another part of me, desired to please my mother to make her proud of me, so she would accept me and love me. Making my mother proud made me proud of myself. Pleasing others was equal to me being accepted and loved. I would please at any cost throughout all of my life. I would easily accommodate the needs of others to obtain this love and acceptance.

The myth of pleasing is related to the myth of self-sacrificing and the myth of over-functioning. I thrived on placing other peoples' needs for nurture and growth, above my own, sacrificing me, in order to make others happy. It gave me a false sense of accomplishment and short-lived emotional comfort. In the moment, I felt super-great being able to help someone, to please someone, to provide pleasure for someone. But, when I was alone, tired and feeling wiped out physically and emotionally, I blamed it on the same people I had helped and on my family. I was tired of helping others and being accommodating to everyone else's needs and desires. It would always be a love hate dynamic because pleasing at any cost had no balance. I had no time for me. I made no time for personal respite and spiritual refreshment. I would have to reprogram myself to think prior to granting someone's request. I began asking myself how does this request affect my time? Is my time in balance? Am I operating in moderation or in over-functioning? God does not require us to please others at any cost. Nor are we commanded to say yes to everything and everyone. If we are to truly serve and be of help to others, we must first take care of ourselves. I learned to do self-care and ask myself, why am I granting a person's request?

> *"Am I now trying to win the approval of human beings, or of God? Or am I trying to please people? If I were still trying to please people, I would not be a servant of Christ."*
>
> —GALATIANS 1:10

These six myths have contributed to who I had become for half of my life. These myths had seeds in my childhood that nurtured my beliefs and methods of functioning. I have totally embraced my myths: of sole responsibility/perfection, rejection, over-functioning, self-sufficiency, sacrificing joy, and pleasing/self-sacrifice. I accept them because they are myths that grew out of my past. I accept them because they are lies, they are untruths. Once I was able to identify, to name and understand my myths, I was able to see what I had become in believing those lies. I was able to understand me as an adult through the eyes of that little girl lost. I was able to see and appreciate that little girl lost. I would never be able to change my past, but I now had the tools to cope with my past so that I could live in my present! I could now reclaim that little girl within, and reclaim who I truly am. I was able to love and embrace that little girl and re-write my myths to rid them the power they had over me. Knowledge equals power!

I was complete and could now think of myself as wonderful! I owed it to God to think of myself as complete and as wonderful. God is my creator. He poured the foundation of his love into my heart, and built the framework of his glory into my bones, designing me with the free will to receive his Son Jesus, and to let his Holy Spirit dwell within my soul. Like an original work of art, a masterpiece, God created me and you with precision love and care, meticulously detailed, putting on those finishing touches making you unique, making you…you! God's creation of you was inventive, ingenious and innovative! He made no one else like you! God gave me and God gave you this precious *love letter* through the words of the Psalmist,

> *"…you hem me in, behind and before; you have laid your hand upon me…For you created my inmost being; you knit me together in my mother's womb. I Praise you because I am fearfully and wonderfully made; your works are wonderful, I know that full well. My frame was not hidden from you when I was woven together in the depths of the earth, your eyes saw my unformed body. All the days ordained for me were written in your book before one of them came to be."*
>
> —PSALM 139:5, 13-16

We are God's beautiful creatures, you and me. God made no junk when he made us intricately woven by his divine strokes. Embracing my past let me embrace me. It let me love me in my imperfectness and vulnerability. I could appreciate the greatness of God's wonder. I could appreciate that I was part of His wonderfulness. This wonderfulness gave me the conviction to embrace my past, live in the present and trust the future. *Like you, I am a work in process striving for progress. Continue in your healing by embracing your past.*

GETTING UNSTUCK STEP BY STEP

STEP 3: EMBRACING YOUR PAST

As you continue in your self-awareness, think about the things that you or others do not like about you. What are your myths? Are you ready to embrace your past? Are you prepared to reclaim your present? Accepting the things that have had a strong negative influence in forming you, can be overwhelming, maybe tempting you to give up on this healing journey. Denial can enter the scene very quickly giving you all the ammunition you need to quit. Hang in there. It is like weight lifting. Your muscles get strengthened as you continue to work them. Do not give in to this tempta-tion. It will only take you two steps backward for every step forward. Once you get over the ugliness with your self-admission, you can re-write those myths. You will be empowered to love your past and live in the present.

Identifying your personal myths

- **IDENTIFY** your personal myths by listening to everyone that you have a relationship with or come in contact with on a daily basis, including your children, no matter their age.

- **EXPLORE** the Why's in your life, in your behavior and thoughts: Ask yourself: Am I defensive? Am I insecure when people talk about me? Do I have problems with acceptance? What makes me impatient or angry? What kind of people do I prefer to be with or stay clear? Why? Am I always the life of the party seeking attention? Why? Am I always the clown, the jokester? Am I always the downer, the serious one? Why?

- **ASK** God to help you identify your myths.

- **BE OPEN** to this self-awareness and don't let it frighten you.

- **OBSERVE** how people respond to you and your presence.

- **THINK** about those that you have asked forgiveness or will ask.

- **EXAMINE** and then determine if there is a pattern.

- **EVALUATE** yourself when you are with other people. What frustrates you or gets you annoyed? Are you aggressive? Are you intimidated by certain types of people? Do you fantasize your myths?

- **REVIEW** *the names* of my six myths and see if any fit you. If not, feel free to name your own myths.

- **ONCE** *you* have identified and named your myths, *write down* how each myth grew from your past and how it has impacted your life and others around you.

Embracing Your Personal Myths

- **ASK** God for strength as you unravel your myths discovering them as obstacles in your self-development and interpersonal relationships.

- **RETURN** to the person that you previously identified as someone you confide in and who is trustworthy for feedback and accountability. This can be more than one person.

- **BEGIN** to embrace your past.

- **LOVE** your past so you can *live completely* in your present and continue in your healing.

Embrace that you are wonderfully made and that God never gave up on you. Rejoice that God is not yet done with you. You are God's wonderful masterpiece!

CHAPTER TEN

RECONCILING YOUR PAST

"Love is patient, love is kind, it is not envious. Love does not brag, it is not puffed up. It is not rude, it is not self-serving, it is not easily angered or resentful...but rejoices in the truth."

—I Corinthians 13:4-6 (NET)

Once Upon A Time

Once upon a time, I once was lost...
And then I found myself.

I once was abandoned...
And now I am no longer alone.

I once had to live by surviving...
And now I just live.

I once strived for perfection...
And now I embrace my imperfection.

I once was blinded by rejection...
And now I see acceptance and love.

Once upon a time, I carried the heavy burden of my past...
And then I released it to God.

I once was bound
And now I am free!

Reconciliation is what got me to the last verse of this poem. After almost two years, I completed my required four units of Clinical Pastoral Education in 2011. My last assignment was to incorporate the re-writing of my myths. I wrote *Once Upon A Time* as part of this requisite. Rewriting my myths was a *declaration* that the chains of my past pains were broken and I am no longer in bondage. Rewriting my myths was a *proclamation* that my past would no longer have the power to destroy my present or my future. Rewriting my myths was the *affirmation* that I no longer hated the little girl of my past and that little girl was no longer lost. Rewriting my myths was a *testimony* that I reconciled my past to God and he will once again fill my mouth with laughter and my lips with shouts of joy. *(Job 8:21)*

To reconcile is to make consistent, to make compatible, to bring to terms, to accept, to conform, and to resolve. To be reconciled is to be in harmony, to be as one. 2 Corinthians 5:18-19 talks about the ministry of reconciliation and how God reconciled us to himself through Christ who died for us and was resurrected. The Greek verb to reconcile, *katallasso*, means "to change thoroughly". When we accept Jesus into our hearts and lives, it becomes our initial reconciliation with God making us one with him, and in him, in harmony with our Creator. We are changed thoroughly. Christ's death reconciled us by delivering us. Reconciliation is the salvation from death to life and does not count our trespasses against us.

Reconciling our past to God is giving the death of our past to God so that we can receive the life that it was meant to be.

Reconciling our past is releasing our past to God with the expectation of rebirth and renewal for our present. Releasing our dark past is letting go of the secrets, the shame, the guilt, the sadness and anger and giving it to the one who can handle it, our heavenly Father. Reconciling our past to God allows us to truly be in harmony with our Creator, because we have truly entrusted him with all of who we are, our past, present and future. Reconciling our past to God is our new birth, because we can breathe without the pain of our past. It means that we can think, talk and share our past as victor instead of victim. I gave my past to God for him to settle, to bring to terms, and to resolve my past. Giving it to God gave me the benefit of peace, giving me the freedom to re-write my myths.

I made *a declaration* that the chains of past pains were broken and that I am now free, and that I refused to succumb to the strongholds of my past. I refused to give in to negative self-prophecy by believing my myths to be true and by using my past as the excuse to justify my bad behavior. It was time for me to no longer conform to the ways of my myths.

> *"Do not conform any longer to the pattern of this world,*
> *but be transformed by the renewing of your mind. Then you*
> *will be able to test and approve what God's will is, his good,*
> *pleasing and perfect will."*
>
> —ROMANS 12:2

It was time for me to grow up emotionally and spiritually.

I made the *proclamation* that I would not give my past the fuel it needed to burn holes in my life. I would not let my myths consume my present and hinder my future. My self-esteem was restored. Self-esteem is the respect and value with which we view ourselves. I acknowledged my past, confronted my past, embraced my past and reconciled my past. I could look at my pain and be okay with it. I could see how I lived with the pain negatively and how I could now live with the past without the pain. I forgave and was forgiven. I had no reason for pain because I was no longer angry, and I no longer believed that I was a victim. I had sincerity in my heart and head when I had forgiven others, and when I had received forgiveness from others, and from God. I truly forgave myself, which liberated me from anger, shame and guilt.

> *"...First be reconciled to your brother, and then come and offer your gift."*
>
> —MATTHEW 5:24

I made the *affirmation* that I accepted and loved me. I was now able to embrace my past, and be at peace with my past by accepting it and loving it. I exchanged the bitter taste of hate for the zest of salt. I rewrote my myths with Godly truths. I replaced sole responsibility/perfection with imperfection/reliance on God. I exchanged rejection for God's love and acceptance as his wonderful creation. I substituted self-sufficiency with dependency on God. I dismissed over-functioning and accepted God's grace of moderation. I substituted sacrificing joy with living life abundantly. I stopped being a superwoman who pleased at all cost, and became a servant of Christ who would first seek God's approval.

I made the *Testimony* that God fills my mouth with laughter and my lips with shouts of joy. I no longer base my existence on the acceptance and love from others. I therefore have no reason to live on the defense fantasizing that I am abandoned and rejected. I no longer view criticism and confrontation as dirty words. I no longer thrive on being busy. Instead I make discerning decisions when to say yes, and when to say no. I decided that is absolutely okay for me to rest, to relax and to refresh myself, and it is definitely okay for me to be silly, to laugh, and to join in the fun on a regular basis. I am liberated from the notion that I am indispensable. I am free to be more dependent on others and on God. I am no longer under the fantasized obligation that I must always pick up the slack, that I must control people and that I must control my environment.

Rewriting my myths and reconciling my past to God was giving me the best gift ever...the gift of peace, and with peace comes an unspeakable joy.

> *"These things I have spoken to you, that my joy may be in you, and that your joy may be full."*
>
> —JOHN 15:11

GETTING UNSTUCK STEP BY STEP

STEP 4: RELEASING YOUR PAST

Rewriting my myths was another part of my healing process. Rewriting my myths did not mean that I would change my way of thinking and behavior overnight. It would be the active participation of reconciling my past to God, not just talking the talk, but walking the walk. In order to do that, I would have to constantly listen to the new tapes in my head, the tapes of my New Truths. I walked most of my life walking in the shoes of my past. It would take patience and daily work to walk the rest of my life in my new shoes. I was okay with this reality. Rewriting your myths is critical in releasing your past to God. Jump in and get going. It's exciting and liberating!

Writing New Truths

- **BEGIN** first by thinking how you want to grow, and how you want to change. What kind of new person do you want to be?

- **WRITE** the new understanding you developed about your myths? How have your myths kept you in bondage?

- **WRITE** how your myths (these lies) have impacted your relationship with God and with others?

- **NOW** that you have this awareness, **WRITE** how will you be different? How will you think different? How will you behave different?

- **RE-WRITE** *your myths* with new truths. Your *New Truths* will include **y**our *declaration, your proclamation, your affirmation* and *your testimony.* Once you have clearly written this, you may put it in the form that best suits your needs. It could be a letter to yourself or to God, or as a poem, a song, or story. It is important to keep them accessible and close to you.

- **ONCE** you have written your *New Truths* read them aloud to yourself and then to your trusted mentor. This is also a way to hold yourself accountable as your walk in your *New Truths*. You will need at least one person to encourage you, to be your cheerleader.

> *"Therefore encourage one another and build each other up, just as in fact you are doing."*
>
> —I Thessalonians 5:11

CHAPTER ELEVEN

WALK IN YOUR BLESSINGS

"...And surely I am with you always to the very end of age."

—Matthew 28:20

WALK

Walk expectantly, knowing that Jesus is walking behind you
Nudging you forward... to be exceedingly fruitful.
Walk assuredly, knowing that Jesus is walking in front of you
Lovingly guiding your footsteps...to a place where you can call home.
Walk confidently, knowing that Jesus is walking by your side,
Giving you the strength...to destroy your myths
and make your new truths a permanent reality.
Walk joyfully, knowing that Jesus is walking with you,
Pouring out his gifts of forgiveness, grace, and mercy...
to shower you with the blessings of
promise, prosperity and peace.

—Rev. D. Blair-Pina ~ 3/5/2015

As we return to the story of Lot and his wife who looked back, who connected with her past and was afraid of the future, we are reminded of what she gave up. Her distraction of staying in the past darkened her perspective. She was not able to acknowledge and appreciate God's blessings by giving up five life-giving promises for her bloodline and future:

1   God had promised Abraham that he would be exceedingly fruitful. (Genesis 17)

2   God had promised Abraham that he would give his present and future offspring, a land to call their own, a place they can call home. (Genesis17)

3   God had promised Abraham that unless ten righteous persons could be found, the city of Sodom would be destroyed. Lot's family totaled six. (Genesis 18)

4   God had promised Lot that he and his family would be able to escape the destruction of Sodom. (Genesis 19)

5   God had promised Lot that he would not have to flee to the mountains and could go instead to the small city of Zoar, which God promised not to destroy. (Genesis 19)

Lot's wife was too preoccupied with the past to recognize the favor that Lot had with God. She did not appreciate the kindness and mercy that God had for her and her family. She did not appreciate Lot's pleading and praying to God to save them, to protect them and to give them a future. She was not willing to trust and follow God's lead to keep moving forward. Before I was able to move forward, to walk toward my future, I had to walk in the present. I had to walk in my current blessings. If I failed to acknowledge my present and failed to appreciate my present, I would be at risk of reverting to those myths and to those dark places in the past. Before I came into my self-awareness, I had moments of depression, moments that grew into days and weeks at a time. I went into these episodes of depression because I did not accept my past. It was easy to talk myself into deep pity parties. I did not understand why I could not change, or why I was angry. I did not understand why it was hard for me to have fun. The more I tuned out the world, the more I grew dark within myself coming out of the present and returning to the woes of my past. I let my myths get the worst of me. I refused to pray, remaining distant from God and from people. I had believed my myths, and believed that I was abandoned and neglected by God. I believed that God did not love me the way he loved others, and that he loved me less. I thought several times about leaving this world. I thought what is the use? Ending my life would be easier. Because I did not stay in communion with God, I was not able to recognize the unseen enemy that delighted in my distance from God and from his truths. The enemy that delighted in me taking my life, and giving up on love, giving up on life's precious moments, giving up on my family and loved ones, and giving up on my precious God and his ministry. This enemy is the Satan that is referred to in Ephesians 6:12.

> *"For our struggle is not against flesh and blood, but against the rulers, against the authorities, against the powers of this dark world and against the spiritual forces of evil in the heavenly realms."*

Once I came out of my self-indulgence and asked the Holy Spirit to help me, and to guide me, I was able to see this enemy and to see how this enemy thrived on my bondage to the pains of my past. I was then able to gird myself against the lies of the Satan with the armor of God, to stand my ground, *with the belt of truth buckled around my waist, with the breastplate of righteousness in place, and with my feet fitted with the readiness that comes from the gospel of peace. In addition to all this, I took up the shield of faith, with which I could extinguish all the flaming arrows of the evil one. I took the helmet of salvation and the sword of the Spirit, which is the word of God.* I found these words in the book of Ephesians, (6:10-18). These words of truth enabled me to be strong in the Lord and his mighty power, by fitting myself for spiritual warfare. Sometimes we have to be in a battle to win the war, and to win the prize. My life, my present, my future and my peace were too precious for me to throw away, and to give into this depression. I would need this full armor of God to get me out of the darkness. I had to keep moving forward to grow in my self-awareness and to walk in my new truths. God's word said to put on that full armor of God to stand against Satan's schemes, to be alert and to pray always. Prayer is simply talking to God. Something so very easy, yet so dynamic and so life changing.

A vast mind embraces change; an ignorant mind fears change; a small mind condemns change. Moving forward requires that we will have to change. We will have to change the way we think and the way we act. Moving forward means being in the present. How do we live in the present? How do we become that new creation that the Apostle Paul taught?

> *"Therefore, if anyone is in Christ, the new creation has come: The old has gone, the new is here!"*
>
> —2 Corinthians 5:17

Living in the present requires that we are *being in the present.* We do this with active reminders to keep us in the present ensuring that we do not react to present circumstances with the mindset and behavior of our past. It requires that we do not give in to the behavior of our myths. Keeping in the present involves us thinking always in our present. The old ideas and scary tales of our past are to stay there…in the past. We learn to constantly renew our minds by constantly asking ourselves the questions, "Why I am feeling this way? What is causing me to respond this way? What am I going to do to change this outcome for the positive in the present context, instead of the negative context of my past?" We renew our minds with mantras like, "I am not the little girl of my painful past, I am the mature adult of my present. I am a new creation, wonderfully made, accepted and loved."

We stay in the present by giving praise and thanks to God for reconciling our past, and for freeing us from its pain. This keeps us in the present, and keeps us appreciative of our present, not taking it for granted. If we *truly appreciate* our present, then we truly, truly, truly have no regrets, and no need for reliving the pains of the past. We can walk in the blessings that God has for us now, living an abundant life in the present. We can move forward freely and confidently towards our future.

> *"But blessed is the one who trusts in the Lord, whose*
> *confidence is in him. They will be like a tree planted by the*
> *water that sends out its roots by the stream…"*

—Jeremiah 17:7-8

GETTING UNSTUCK STEP BY STEP

STEP 5: MOVING FORWARD

Do you know who you are? How do you identify yourself in the present? How do you describe yourself in the present? Now that you have written your New Truths, you have to activate those new truths with a daily commitment of verbal reminders and prayers. How is God calling you to be in the present?

> *"So then, just as you received Christ Jesus as Lord, continue to live in him, rooted and built up in him, strengthened in the faith as you were taught, and overflowing with thankfulness.*
>
> —COLOSSIANS 2:6-7

- **RELEASE** all of you to God. If you have not asked Jesus into your life to be your savior and to be the Lord of your life, now is the time. You gave your past to God, now give him your present, and give him your future, so that he can give you eternal life.

- **SAY** these words, "God, forgive me for my sins. I invite you into my life and I accept your son Jesus, who died, was crucified and rose from the dead just for me." Amen, it is done!

- **WRITE** a paragraph about who you are in the present, answering the above questions.

- **WRITE** a **WEEKLY REFLECTION.** You will reflect on how you are *being in the present* and how you are walking in your New Truths. How are you dealing with triggers? How are you able to talk about your past and relating it to others? Are you still emotionally charged when you talk about your past, or is it becoming less emotional and easier to discuss, and to remember? Your weekly reflection can be two sentences or three pages. Whatever you desire or need is totally up to you. If you miss a week no problem. This is good exercise until you are able to express and to deal with your past in the present as the present you, not the person you were in your past.

- **PRAY** to God, talk to God, ask God for direction, and thank God for your present, and for your present blessings. Keep on the armor of God.

- **WALK** In your present blessings.

- **MOVE FORWARD** toward your future blessings.

Pray continually.

—1 THESSALONIANS 5:17

CHAPTER TWELVE

DON'T LOOK BACK

*"Jesus turned, and seeing her he said, Take heart, daughter;
your faith has made you well..."*

—MATTHEW 9:22

DO YOU HEAR ME?

*I Know that your mind is tired,
your body weary,
and your soul weakened.
I love you, my daughter...like no one else.
I can fix you. I can deliver you. I can make you strong.
Do you believe me?
Do you hear me daughter?
I made you. You are amazing!
You are free!
Do you believe me?
Do you hear me daughter?
Your mind is no longer tired, but revived in the wisdom of my word!
Your body is no longer worn, but refreshed in the fountain of fulfillment!*

Your soul is no longer weakened, but restored in the strength of the Spirit!
Do you hear me daughter?
You are free!
Yes, my Father, I hear you!
I am free!

—Rev. D. Blair-Pina
1/10/1998

My journey of acknowledging my past, confronting my past, embracing my past, releasing my past and moving forward has been exhausting and difficult…and it will be for you as well. I continue in this journey because I still have work to do.

"In the same way, faith by itself, if it is not accompanied by action, is dead."

—James 2:17

I still have to monitor and keep my frustration at bay so it does not rise to anger. I am well aware of where it came from and how it surfaces, but I now have to break the habit of reacting to certain circumstances. By constantly walking in the present and keeping myself accountable, I am able to move forward. Keeping yourself accountable is vital. If you fall back, don't worry, you can get back on track. It is like losing weight. If you don't ever refer back to the scale, then you risk gaining much more weight. The one or two pounds easily turn into ten and twenty pounds, and before you know it, you have gone back further. Even if the truth hurts, it is far better to step on the scale, see the results and deal with it now!

This journey requires your commitment. Walking in your New Truths and keeping your myths from resurfacing involves you getting on the scale frequently to check your progress. Check your progress by writing a weekly reflection, by asking yourself questions, by evaluating yourself and by talking with your supportive mentor. If you have a bad day then try to do better the next day. Just make sure to never go dark, to go off the radar screen when you have tough periods. No matter how you feel, make sure to stay in contact with your trusted friend or mentor. Stay in touch with the Lord of your life, so you can consecrate your life afresh, so you can tap into your inner strength and rest in his Spirit.

> *"… Come to me, all who labor and are heavy laden, and I will give you rest. Take my yoke upon you, and learn from me, for I am gentle and lowly in heart, and you will find rest for your souls. For my yoke is easy, and my burden is light."*
>
> —Matthew 11:28-3

The rewards of this journey are countless. For how can we really count the blessings from God? I have made many major and minor improvements in addressing my past issues. I can speak about my past without the intensity of sadness. I have learned to appreciate laughter and work on coming out of my awkwardness. I no longer feel the compulsion to clean my house every waking moment. (Amen!) I have come very far in believing that I am accepted rather than rejected. I have learned to appreciate my past and to take from it the good that I can, to further my self-awareness and to help others.

> *"And we know that in all things God works for the good of those who love him, who have been called according to his purpose."*
>
> —Romans 8:28

I am able to keep alive my New Truths by walking in the present with thanksgiving. The alternative is negativity which brings nothing but doubt and discouragement. Looking back is a distraction that slows us down and immobilizes us.

Healing works best in an environment of positivity and the best way to heal is to move forward. There is no reason to wake up to the glass half empty. It is far more refreshing to drink from a glass half full! I wake up every morning with the attitude that this morning I will be positive, I will be glad and full of joyful expectations. This has been my mantra for two years because I appreciate each day that God gives me. It is my new day, my new beginning, my new birth. Make every morning your new day, your new beginning, your new birth.

> *This is the day that the Lord has made; let us rejoice and be glad in it. O Lord, save us; O Lord, grant us success.*
>
> —PSALM 118:24-25

As long as God gives you the breath to breathe, you have been given another day to begin a second chance. What joy to know that we have every morning to start again, one day at a time, walking by faith not by sight.

> *"Now faith is confidence in what we hope for and assurance about what we do not see."*
>
> —HEBREWS 11:1

When you are tempted to look back and to go to the dark places of pain, you must *resist, refocus* and *redirect*. Resist the myths of your past. Refocus with your renewed mind and with your new truths. Redirect your longing, your thirst, to be in the present and to stay in the present.

"Jesus said to her, "Everyone who drinks of this water will be thirsty again, but whoever drinks of the water that I will give him will never be thirsty again. The water that I will give him will become in him a spring of water welling up to eternal life."

—JOHN 4:13-14

Yes, I am victorious! Yes, I am free! Yes, my Lord has brought me from dark to light, and Yes, I have put the past behind me. I don't need to look back! I refuse to let my past consume me.

"Let all bitterness and wrath and anger and clamor and slander be put away from you, along with all malice. Be kind to one another, tenderhearted, forgiving one another, as God in Christ forgave you."

—EPHESIANS 4:31-32

Put the past behind, and don't ever look back, because your future depends on it!

CHAPTER THIRTEEN

WHERE IS YOUR ZOAR?

"This is what the Lord says,
he who made a way through the sea,
a path through the mighty waters,
who drew out the chariots and horses,
the army and reinforcements together,
and they lay there, never to rise again,
extinguished, snuffed out like a wick:
Forget the former things; do not dwell on the past.
See, I am doing a new thing.
Now it springs up; do you not perceive it?
I am making a way in the desert
and streams in the wasteland.
The wild animals honor me,
the jackals and the owls,
because I provide water in the desert
and streams in the wasteland,
to give drink to my people, my chosen,
the people I formed for myself
that they may proclaim my praise."

—Isaiah 43:16-19

Lot's rescue was a result of prayer. His request for shelter in the nearby town of Zoar, was granted by God. God showed Lot favor by promising to save him and his family, and to not destroy Zoar. Zoar was located near the mouth of a large peninsula. It was far enough away from the destroyed plains of Sodom and Gomorrah. God had wiped out and burned those cities to start fresh. The small town of Zoar would have water to cultivate the land. It would be their new home to start over.

Their future was waiting, and your future is waiting. Where is your Zoar? Your Zoar is your new life in your new walk, as a new creation. Where do you want to be a year from now... emotionally and spiritually? Where do you want to be five years from now? What about your aspirations? God will take you to your Zoar. The only thing that will get in the way of your future, is your past.

Do you trust God with your future? Do you trust God to take you to your Zoar? I trusted God with my future. I trusted God to move me from my pains to my gains.

> " For I know the plans I have for you," declares the Lord,
> "plans to prosper you and not to harm you, plans to give you
> hope and a future. Then you will call on me and come and
> pray to me, and I will listen to you. You will seek me and find
> me when you seek me with all your heart. I will be found by
> you," declares the Lord..."
>
> —JEREMIAH 29:11–14

In the period that God has you in a holding position as he grows you toward your future, water your wait with patience and with endurance. When God gives you that open door, head for your Zoar! Conceptualize your future! Visualize your future! Energize your future! Materialize your future! See it, believe it, prepare for it, then make it happen!

My burden was finally lifted! It took me twenty-six years to put my past in God's hand. It took me getting through my "five steps to my future" to also give my present and my future to God. God my Heavenly Father and Divine Creator who knew what it would take for me to arrive at that place, a place where he could do a new thing in me, a place to call my new home, a place in the desert where he made streams in my wasteland. Because God did that for me, I was able to pass along my journey to you, so that you… shall do the same for someone else!

> *"… he saved us, not because of righteous things we had done, but because of his mercy. He saved us through the washing of rebirth and renewal by the Holy Spirit."*

> —Titus 3:5

FIVE STEPS TO YOUR FUTURE

"Since we live by the Spirit, let us keep in step with the Spirit."

—GALATIANS 5:25

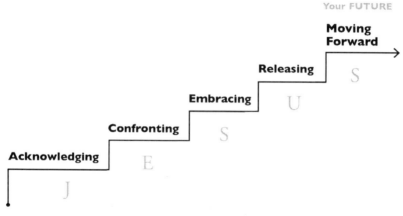

Getting Unstuck Step By Step

Your FUTURE

Moving Forward

Releasing

Embracing

Confronting

Acknowledging

J E S U S

Your PAST

*"May God Bless You As You Continue Your Journey.
May You Walk With Assurance, May You Grow With Grace,
May You Rest In His Perfect Peace, And May You Be
Comforted By His Love."*

—REVEREND D. BLAIR-PINA

ABOUT THE AUTHOR

Reverend Dyanne Blair-Pina is an Associate Pastor at Christ Fellowship Baptist Church in Brooklyn, New York. She was born and reared in Boston, Massachusetts. She received her B.S. in Broadcasting & Film from Boston University. After working as producer for the City of Austin Municipal Access Channel, she left the cable television industry and entered the social service community as outreach worker, advocate and educator for various community organizations including the National Black Leadership Initiative on Cancer, the Coalition for Addiction Pregnancy and Parenting, The Alliance of Young Families, Boston and the Boston Healthy Start Initiative Consortium (BHSI) which was instrumental in the landmark initiative of the development of the Infant Mortality Project.

Her love for helping people inspired her to accept roles with the American Cancer Society, The Medical Foundation, and the Boston Team Harmony Foundation which brought together at its annual event 10,000 diverse high school students to peaceably take a stand against racism and bigotry. Keynote speakers like former United States Secretary of State, Hillary Rodham Clinton, Reverend Bernice King, and Congressman John Lewis, passed on courage and inspiration to these youths.

Reverend Blair-Pina earned her Master of Divinity degree from Fuller Theology Seminary. Her coursework concentration was in homiletics and family counseling. She was ordained at the First Baptist Church of Los Angeles where she received her license to preach. Reverend Blair-Pina has provided spiritual care as a regional hospice chaplain and as a hospital chaplain for tier one trauma centers. She founded the O.A.I.S.I.S139 ministry, a ministry of creative self-expression that offers emotional healing to women who have been abused, abandoned and unloved. Reverend Blair-Pina was recently asked to advise the Massachusetts Women of Faith Committee, which empowers women of faith to stand up collectively for their political, social and religious agenda.

Reverend Blair-Pina is available for seminars, workshops and keynote speaking engagements to share the biblical principles and applications from her book,
Stuck in the Past Can Get You Burned.

Contact information: *rev.dministries@gmail.com*